The Big Ten
A Study of the
Ten Commandments

Phillip A. Ross

Pilgrim Platform
Marietta, Ohio

ISBN: 978-0-9820385-3-6

Published by

Pilgrim Platform
149 E. Spring St., Marietta
Ohio, 45750
www.pilgrim-platform.org

Biblical quotations are from the *Modern King James Bible*, Jay Green, Jr., Sovereign Grace Publishers, 1993, unless otherwise cited.

Printed in the United States of America

For cousin Mark
a fellow traveler

TABLE OF CONTENTS

INTRODUCTION

We live in an age of increasing lawlessness. It is not simply that there is a void of law, far from it. Quite the opposite is actually true. There is an overwhelming preponderance of laws, the size, scope and complexity of which the world has never before seen. The body of law for any modern country, and in particular the United States—the most litigious society in history—is phenomenal. There are laws for everything. No one can keep up with the constant flood of laws produced by every body that is capable of law making. People everyday violate laws they have never heard of. So, how can I say that we live in an age of increasing lawlessness?

What is in view here is not human law, but *God's law*. Just to speak the phrase brings a chill upon many a backbone. People don't like to talk about God's law. To do so is to be branded a fundamentalist, legalist, theonomist and/or extremist, all in the most vile sense possible. For the most part contemporary Christians believe that they have arrived at a time in history that is beyond the application of any Old Testament laws, and in many cases, a time that is beyond all biblical law. People have converted the gospel of grace to mean a gospel without law—without obligation or responsibility. The good news that is preached in too many pulpits today is lawlessness, couched in terms of a gospel of positive thinking, of upbeat moralisms intended to make life better, richer, fuller, more meaningful, and happier. In order to justify the human distaste for biblical law, people —Christians among them—no longer speak of God's law or the human obligation to it, not even in Bible study or worship.

However, the Bible is not a divided witness. It is a whole, a unity. God's Word, God's testimony is completely true. No part of it contradicts any other part. All parts are true and applicable to faith and life. There are two testaments, but only one God. The God of the Old Testament is none other than Jesus Christ, the Messiah of God. This understanding of Scripture is not new, but it has fallen on hard times. Thus, as it is resurrected in these pages it will no doubt seem odd or foreign

—even heretical to many Christians who have forgotten their own roots. How I wish it were not so!

These chapters were originally sermons for a home fellowship. They have been reworked to make them more generally applicable. They are intended to be foundational for a proper understanding of biblical Christianity. They are neither comprehensive, nor complete; neither systematic, nor extemporaneous. They are, however, intended to address issues of orthodoxy and error that plague modern society and the contemporary churches. They are neither scholarly nor popular in style or content. They simply expose the Bible for what it is, and apply it to the world in which we live. Though these insights and applications will distress many people, they are an honest effort to represent Scripture in and of itself, apart from ideology and the subtle influences known as political correctness. It is an effort in the Spirit of Jesus, who asked the Pharisees, "Why do you also transgress the commandment of God by your tradition?" (Matthew 15:3). There is no intention to produce a traditional denominational or theological perspective, but rather to cut through the kind of denominational and theological baggage that so blinds contemporary Christians.

I am indebted to those who endure my preaching and feeble efforts to get at God's truth, and pray that these pages will not be an unnecessary burden to those who still seek God's truth in these days of darkness and blindness. Come, Lord Jesus!

Phillip A. Ross
October, 2001

It is amazing how time flies. Seven years have passed since completing this manuscript. I have made some minor revisions to it and put it into a standard layout format, and now offer it to a wider audience in the hope that it will be useful to the Lord.

I treat some of Scripture's "hard sayings," but I have tried to insure that they belong to Scripture and are not part of my own peculiarities. Of course, my peculiarities will color them—and everything else, and so I pray for your understanding, forgiveness and persistence to wrangle God's truth from my words.

Phillip A. Ross
Marietta, Ohio
April, 2008

BY WHAT AUTHORITY?

Why do you attend church? By what authority do God's churches gather together? What's the purpose? What difference does it really make? And, regardless of your answers, how do you know that what you think is actually right? Does being right really mean anything?

The Old Testament word for authority is *yad*, which means *hand*. There are many idioms related to the hand. For instance, the phrase "into (or under) someone's hand" means responsibility, care, and dominion over that person. Here is the responsibility, for instance, of Sarah over Hagar, of Joseph over Potiphar's house, of Moses and Aaron over Israel, of King David over his kingdom. Similarly, God has this kind of authority over His people, who place themselves under His care, His authority, His *hand*.

The many uses of the word or idea of *hand* are quite interesting because they are so varied. It is amazing how many different thoughts are associated with *hand*.

To be "delivered into someone's hands" is to be defeated by them. Christians, who are delivered by Jesus Christ—saved—surrender themselves to God in response to their salvation. To be "delivered out of someone's hands" is to be spared. This is not contradictory but suggests that being delivered *into* God's hands is to be delivered *out of* Satan's hands. In Scripture, the hand symbolized power and strength, means and action. "Though he fall," writes the Psalmist, "he shall not be utterly cast down; For the Lord upholds him with His hand" (Psalm 37:24).

The phrase "in one's hands" means possession. The old adage said, "A bird in the hand is worth two in the bush." To have something "in hand" is to own or control it. To be in God's hands is to be His possession. "To give one's hands under" someone else means to submit to them. "To stretch out the hand" generally means to attack or hit. "To put one's hands to" something means to work on it. "To strengthen the hands of" someone means to help them, to increase

3

their power and/or holdings. And obstinate rebellion is often characterized by "high handedness."

"To lay hands on" someone has at least four different connotations. First, it can mean to kill or injure someone. When Joseph was put into the pit by his brothers, "Reuben said to them, 'Shed no blood, but cast him into this pit which is in the wilderness, and do not lay a hand on him'" (Genesis 37:22). In other words, do not hit or hurt him.

Second, it has been used in ritual ceremonies conferring blessing. "Now when Joseph saw that his father laid his right hand on the head of Ephraim, it displeased him; so he took hold of his father's hand to remove it from Ephraim's head to Manasseh's head" (Genesis 48:17). This kind of laying on of hands conferred a blessing.

Third, it has been used to commission a person for a particular office or task. "As they ministered to the Lord and fasted, the Holy Spirit said, 'Now separate to Me Barnabas and Saul for the work to which I have called them.' Then, having fasted and prayed, and laid hands on them, they sent them away." Here the laying on of hands confers not only blessing, but power and authority.

Fourth, it was used to convey the theological concept of substitution. On the Day of Atonement the high priest transferred Israel's sins to a goat, a substitute sacrifice (Exodus 29:10-19). Similarly, to be delivered into Christ's hands indicates the reception of Christ's substitutionary atonement on the cross for one's own sin (Colossians 2:14). Here the laying on of hands by the high priest conferred not blessing or power, but sin and guilt. Through the laying on of hands came a transfer, an exchange.

In worship the saints raise their hands to God. "Hear the voice of my supplications When I cry to You, When I lift up my hands toward Your holy sanctuary" (Psalms 28:2). Paul called upon "men (to) pray everywhere, lifting up holy hands, without wrath and doubting" (1 Timothy 2:8). Thus, in a general sense the word *hand* means authority, but it is an active authority not a passive authority. It is not mere authority, but authority with the power to act. The use of the word *hand* to define authority suggests that biblical authority was a kind of decision-making that resulted in the accomplishment of something. In the case of biblical authority God's will is accomplished by God's authority. And the bible teaches that all authority is derived from God, or is based upon God's absolute authority.

The Greek word for *authority* (*exousia*) means the liberty of doing as one pleases. To do as one pleases requires having the power of authority or influence, and the power of right or privilege. Generally speaking, authority means the power to rule or govern. Authority implies the ability to set or make law. It is the power of leaders whose wishes and commands must be obeyed. Of course, no one has ultimate authority except God Himself. Thus, human authority is always a derived authority and is divided into various areas of application or kinds of authorities, or jurisdictions. A jurisdiction provides certain fixed limits within which a particular authority may be exercised. Jurisdiction—the right to have a particular authority in a particular case or area—always limits the extent of the various authorities.

A synonym for authority is *power*. And *power* is defined as the ability or capacity to accomplish something or to act effectively. Thus, authority is not simply the barking of commands, but requires the ability to carry out or execute those commands. If I harp on my children to clean their rooms, but they fail to do so, then, my parental authority has been denied or broken because my authority failed to accomplish its stated purpose. In this case while I think I may have authority, I don't because my command accomplished nothing.

Here we can see that the power of authority is not simply a possession of the person who commands it. The parent commanded that the room be cleaned, but it didn't happen. Thus, the parent's authority was in vain. It was powerless, and therefore, was not authority at all. Authority, in order to be effective, must be acknowledged by those who stand under it. If the lieutenants do not obey the captain, then the captain's authority is ineffective. He may as well not have any authority. The effective power of authority must be given (bestowed or acknowledged) by those who are under it.

Thus, human authority, in order to be effective, cannot be merely imposed from the top, but must be bestowed or honored from the bottom up. It must be honored and respected enough to result in obedience, or it is not authority. The authority or power of a king is not established by his military or political might alone, but for the kingdom to be successful (long lived, sustainable) the authority of the king must also be accepted by the willing obedience or respect that is given to him by his subjects. Apart from obedience to commands authority is meaningless. There is no authority without the means and ability to enforce one's authority. Without teeth, authority is at best merely influence, and at worst delusion.

Divine Authority

God's power, however, is established upon a different basis. God's power is a given in the universe. God speaks and it is done (Genesis 1:3). God's will shall be done, period, no ifs, ands or buts. And yet the establishment of Christ's power and authority on earth, the establishment of His authority in the hearts and lives of his people produces the faith and obedience of His people. There is no question that Christ's people will obey Him. They can do no other—not because they are unable, nor because of some misunderstood irresistibility, but because they do not want to disobey their Lord. God's people want what God wants, and work to enact it.

However, the establishment of Christian authority, biblical authority—church authority—in the hearts and minds of God's people is not merely a top-down enforcement of God's domination, though such enforcement is not beyond God's abilities. Rather, God has decreed a bottom-up acquiescence to the authority of God's will as found in Scripture as a matter of love and appreciation (Deuteronomy 6:5, Matthew 22:37). God does not shove His authority down the throats of His people, though He can and does sometimes chastise them for their own good. Rather, God's people willingly acknowledge and submit to His authority of their own free will. When God's authority is exercised through human agency, as it often is, it operates as authority honored and bestowed by believers rather than imposed by the Lord. Christians willingly submit to the structures of God's authority, just as those who reject it do so willingly.

Let's trace the major uses of the word *authority* (*exousia*) in the New Testament. Matthew tells us that Jesus "taught them as one having authority, and not as the scribes" (Matthew 7:29). The authority of Jesus was recognized by His people. Sheep naturally recognize the voice and the authority of their shepherd. Later, Jesus commended the authority of the Centurion for his faithfulness, which was based upon the Centurion's understanding of authority. Jesus honored the Centurion's understanding of authority. The Centurion said, "For I also am a man under authority, having soldiers under me. And I say to this one, 'Go,' and he goes; and to another, 'Come,' and he comes; and to my servant, 'Do this,' and he does it" (Matthew 8:9). The Centurion understood that authority requires obedience.

Not everyone recognized Jesus' authority. The Pharisees and Sadducees challenged Jesus' authority on more than one occasion. "Now when He came into the temple, the chief priests and the elders of the people confronted Him as He was teaching, and said, 'By what authority are You doing these things? And who gave You this authority?'" (Matthew 21:23). The Pharisees and scribes acknowledged Jesus' authority in a back-handed way. They suggested, not only the fact that Jesus had authority, but that His authority was other than—not related to—their own. By not recognizing Christ's authority, they testified to the fact of their own opposition and disobedience to God's authority.

The resurrected Christ appeared to the disciples and gave them the Great Commission, saying, "All authority has been given to Me in heaven and on earth. Go therefore and make disciples of all the nations, baptizing them in the name of the Father and of the Son and of the Holy Spirit, teaching them to observe all things that I have commanded you; and lo, I am with you always, even to the end of the age" (Matthew 28:18-20). All authority is God's authority, and all has been given to Christ. Thus, even what we might call secular or pagan governmental authority belongs to God. Paul taught, "Let every soul be subject to the governing authorities. For there is no authority except from God, and the authorities that exist are appointed by God" (Romans 13:1). If Paul could say this about pagan Rome, then we are certainly are under obligation to live in obedience to our government!

CHURCH AUTHORITY

There is a special authority that sustains Christ's church. That authority originates in God's Word as it is taught and illuminated by church leaders, and acknowledged by the people of the church—in continuity with the historic teaching of the evangelical and Reformed churches through the ages and informed by the presence and power of the Holy Spirit, of course. Paul, a leader of Christ's church, had such authority as is evidenced by 1 Corinthians 9:18, "What is my reward then? That when I preach the gospel, I may present the gospel of Christ without charge, that I may not abuse my authority in the gospel." Paul was saying that biblical authority cannot be bought or sold, but is always conferred by the Holy Spirit and honored by God's people. It is also important that such authority not be abused. Church authority, like all of the various God-given authorities, must recognize and operate only within the limitations of its own jurisdiction.

What is the purpose of biblical authority in the church? Paul said that it was given to church leaders "for edification, and not for destruction" (2 Corinthians 10:8). To edify is to instruct or to make someone understand something. In particular, it is to instruct in order to encourage the intellectual, moral, or spiritual improvement of God's people. To edify means to teach. Thus, God's authority in the church provides the authority to teach Scripture, as well as to learn and practice obedience to Scripture. God's people gather for the purpose of worship, which involves teaching and learning. The point is that worship occurs on the basis of biblical authority alone.

Are there biblical limitations upon church authority? Are their limitations regarding the various kinds of authorities? There are. One of them that has given churches much difficulty involves the roles and responsibilities of women. It is an important issue and is dealt with forthrightly in Scripture. Thus, it behooves us to study it and to willingly abide by it.

Regarding this issue Paul wrote to Timothy, "I do not permit a woman to teach or to have authority over a man, but to be in silence"

(1 Timothy 2:12). The first thing to notice is that the Greek word for *authority* here is not *exousia*, but *authenteo*, which means to usurp or assume authority. Women are not to usurp authority. Then again, no one is to usurp authority. It does not mean that women have no biblical authority at all. Nor does it mean that women have no authority in the church. Nor does it mean that women cannot teach. Rather, it means that biblical or church authority—teaching authority—is not self-conferred. It is inappropriate for women or anyone else to assume or usurp authority of any kind for themselves.

FAMILY AUTHORITY

The first unit in which biblical authority is defined and granted is the family unit. There the husband/father is to be the head of the household, and the wife/mother is to be his helper in the accomplishment of God's purpose for their union. God's fundamental purpose is defined in Genesis 1:28 as human dominion of the earth for the glory of God. That mandate rests primarily upon the family because it was given to the family prior to the establishment of God's church or any form of extra-family government. But it is not for the family alone, but rather it is for the family in the midst of the other God-given authorities: personal conscience, family, church and civil.

The basic story of the Old Testament pertains to the lesson that God's people are not based upon family or blood ties, but on grace. The establishment of the Jewish theocracy and its various abuses served to teach us the errors of believing that God's "chosen people" are a particular race or extended blood family. They are not and never have been. Paul discussed this in Romans 9. It was a hard lesson then, and it is still a hard lesson, as evidenced by the lack of preaching on Romans 9 today.

Jesus later redefined God's family, not as a biological unit, but as a social structure built upon the grace of God and fellowship between "brothers and sisters" (related by regeneration) who have been born-again in Christ. Paul clarified that the Christian family was structured like the biological family, with the husband/father as the head and the wife/mother as the helper. Thus, men were to provide primary leadership for the church as for the family, and women were not to usurp or assume for themselves positions of authority in the church that were not given to them first by the heads of their own households, and secondly by the leaders of the church. That doesn't mean that women can't teach or that women can't serve in the church. Remember, church leadership is service not domination (Matthew 20:25-26).

All Christian authority is derived authority. It is authority in submission to a greater authority—wives to their husbands, church people to their church leaders, church leaders to Scripture. All Christians are to live in submission to God through Christ as revealed in Scripture and empowered by the Holy Spirit, and within the structures of authority in which they find themselves—family, church, and state. Christians are to bloom where they are planted.

Both Peter and Jude addressed this issue of usurping authority. Peter wrote about "those who walk according to the flesh in the lust of uncleanness and despise authority. They are presumptuous, self-willed" (2 Peter 2:10). Presumption and self-will are to be avoided personally and in all matters of biblical authority. Peter used a different Greek word for authority, the same word used in Jude 1:8, "Likewise also these dreamers defile the flesh, reject authority, and speak evil of dignitaries." The word used here was *kuriotes*, which contains the root of the Greek word for Lord (*kurios*) suggesting divine authority or Lordship. Peter and Jude both noted that the authority that was being rejected by some people in their day was Christ's authority or Lordship over His people—biblical authority.

What defines God's people as God's people is their faith or belief in Jesus Christ as the Messiah of God who brings them into willing and joyful submission to God's authority, biblical authority. To be a child of God is to relish—to love and wholeheartedly desire to live in obedience to—God's authority, God's Word. To gather as a people of God is to gather under God's authority, biblical authority. Upon this foundation —the foundation of the authority of God's Word—Christian families and churches of Christ are governed. And apart from this foundation, God's people are delivered into the hand of Satan.

Biblical Authority

Thus, Christians gather under the authority of Scripture, but they must clarify what parts of Scripture are authoritative. Are Christians under the authority of the Old Testament? Or the New? Are just the words of Jesus authoritative? Christians are under all of it! Because Christians claim the inerrancy and infallibility of Scripture, they claim that *all* of the words of Scripture are authoritative, both the Old Testament and the New. Our task is to understand all of Scripture as best we are able in the light of the history of the Christian church, and to apply it to our lives, our families, and our fellowship with one another.

Because the lives of the faithful are lives of repentance, God's people live in repentance. The new millennium provides an opportunity to rethink, to reevaluate everything that we think and do, to repudiate what is not according to God's authority and to reaffirm what is. We have an opportunity and an obligation to repent and rethink everything we understand and think we understand, to reevaluate everything in the light of God's Word, personally, as families, and as a people of God. This is the opportunity that God has given us in the midst of our circumstance. This is the purpose for which God has called us together.

HEADS UP, HATS OFF

*To the woman He said, I will greatly increase your sorrow and your
conception. In pain you shall bear sons, and your desire shall be
toward your husband, and he shall rule over you.*   —Genesis 3:16

*If you do well, shall you not be accepted? And if you do not do well,
sin crouches at the door; and its desire is for you, and you shall rule
over it.*   —Genesis 4:7

*Wives, submit yourselves to your own husbands, as to the Lord. For
the husband is the head of the wife, even as Christ is the head of the
church; and He is the Savior of the body.*   —Ephesians 5:22-23

God's curse was the result of Adam's sin. God cursed the serpent,
the woman and Adam, and through Adam God's curse extended
to the ground. The woman's curse was certainly the least of the
three, in terms of significance, extent, and the literal number of
verses describing it. The woman was given two things to deal with,
pain in childbirth and submission to her husband. "To the woman He
said: 'I will greatly multiply your sorrow and your conception; In pain
you shall bring forth children; Your desire shall be for your husband,
And he shall rule over you'" (Genesis 3:16). No consequence of the Fall
ever negated the creation mandate that the wife was to be a helper to
the husband (Genesis 2:18). The husband's rule over his wife was reiterated after the Fall and again later in the New Testament.

Cast out of the Garden, Adam and Eve had two sons, Cain and
Abel. "Abel was a keeper of sheep, but Cain was a tiller of the ground"
(Genesis 4: 2). Abel was younger, Cain older. "And in the process of
time it came to pass that Cain brought an offering of the fruit of the

ground to the Lord. Abel also brought of the firstborn of his flock and of their fat. And the Lord respected Abel and his offering, but He did not respect Cain and his offering. And Cain was very angry, and his countenance fell" (Genesis 4:3-5).

GOD'S PLAN

Why did the Lord respect Abel's offering and reject Cain's? Because from the very beginning God planned to save the world through the blood sacrifice of the Lamb of God, Jesus Christ. Thus, from the very beginning God's salvation plan pointed to and unfolded toward this purpose. Abel's offering from his flock of sheep symbolized God's plan. Cain's offering of fruit did not. By analogy, fruit, produced in the lives of believers by the Holy Spirit, was the *result* of salvation, not its *cause*.

There was nothing about or in Cain or Abel, nothing about their respective characters, nor regarding their obedience, that had any effect upon God's preference of Abel's offering over Cain's. God didn't approve the one and disapprove the other because of anything in or about these brothers. God approved of one and disapproved of the other because of His salvation plan and the necessary symbolism that would set up God's plan and purpose in history. All of history would point to the atonement provided by the Lamb of God, Jesus Christ.

God's preference had nothing to do with Cain or Abel as individuals. It was not about them. Rather, God's preference had to do with God's salvation plan—salvation by grace through faith alone. Yet, Cain became distressed, and his distress focused upon God's preference for Abel's offering. Cain became "very angry" (v. 4) at God and at his brother, Abel. So, God addressed him, "Why are you angry? And why has your countenance fallen? If you do well, will you not be accepted? And if you do not do well, sin lies at the door. And its desire is for you, but you should rule over it" (Genesis 4:6-7).

Here we have what may be called the Covenant of Works, given not to Adam, but to Adam's son, Cain. If you do well, God said to Cain, you will be accepted. Salvation is about being accepted by God. Thus, Cain's salvation depended upon his—Cain's—doing well, his performance, his works or behavior in the world. If Cain failed to "do well," then sin would overwhelm him. The KJV personifies sin, "sin lieth at the door. And unto thee shall be his desire, and thou shalt rule over him" (v. 7). God commanded Cain to "rule over" sin. The clear implication is that if Cain did not take charge over sin, sin would take charge over him, and lead him into destruction.

In the same sense, God gave the husband charge over his wife, lest she have charge over him and lead them both into destruction. Again, the issue concerns God's salvation plan, not the abilities of the husband or the wife. Cain was to "rule over" his sin as Adam was to "rule over" Eve. But why should a husband have charge over his wife and not his wife over him? Indeed, the same question applies in the same way to Cain and Able.

Why did Abel's sacrifice please God? Why did Cain's not please Him? Not because of anything in or about Cain or Abel, nor did God set Adam over Eve because of anything about them personally, nor anything about men or women generally, but because it served His salvation plan, and the other way didn't. It had nothing to do with male superiority or female inferiority, nothing to do with the inherent value of one person over another or of men over women, but only with God's salvation plan. The bottom line is that it is that way because that's the way God wants it. Is it enough that God said it, that God wants it that way, or do we want to argue with God?

It is the same issue that led to the Fall in the first place. God forbade eating from the tree of the knowledge of good and evil. Why? What does one fruit matter over another? God forbade it, isn't that enough? The issue isn't whether we understand God's purpose, but whether we will obey God's commands. God made Adam to rule over Eve. God preferred the offering of Abel's lamb over Cain's fruit. God commanded Cain to rule over his sin. God sent Jesus Christ. God didn't bring any of these things about because of any superior or inferior characteristics of any of the people involved. Rather, all of these things are the result of God's grace, not man's character or abilities.

GOD'S PLAN IS STILL IN EFFECT

Were any of these things changed anywhere in the Old Testament or in the New? They were not. Nowhere in either Testament were any of these changed. Women were continually to be subject to their husbands, God continued to prefer the sacrifice of the Lamb, and sinful man was commanded to rule over his sin. Jesus Christ is Messiah forever.

Paul wrote to the church at Ephesus, "Wives, submit to your own husbands, as to the Lord. For the husband is head of the wife, as also Christ is head of the church; and He is the Savior of the body" (Ephesians 5:22-23). Here the structure of the family is reiterated and applied to the church. As the husband is the head or authority of the wife, so Christ is the head or authority of the husband. The husband is the head of the family, and Christ is the head of the church. The authority structures of each—family and church—are identical. The church is subject to Christ as wives are subject to their husbands in everything.

Does this mean that husbands are free to do whatever they want? Not at all. Husbands are subject to Christ as Jesus Christ was subject to God. Jesus said, "I can of Myself do nothing. As I hear, I judge; and My judgment is righteous, because I do not seek My own will but the will of the Father who sent Me" (John 5:30). So it is with men—faithful husbands and fathers. They are not free to do whatever they want, but must live in submission to Christ. The alternative to living in submission to Christ is Cain's alternative. "If you do well, will you not be accepted? And if you do not do well, sin lies at the door. And its desire is for you, but you should rule over it" (Genesis 4:6-7). By God's grace Christ deals with the sin that lies at the Christian's door. Apart from Christ people must wrestle with sin themselves, under their own strength and power. In Christ, however, sin is covered, paid for, defeated—choose your analogy.

God doesn't require anything from His people. He knows our weaknesses and our frailties. He knows that we cannot conquer sin ourselves. He knows that Satan is stronger than we are. He knows that sin will defeat us every time. That's why He set His salvation plan in motion. That's why He sent His Son to defeat Satan and save His people. That's why He sends His Holy Spirit to be our guide and stay, our strength and protection.

God gave Adam and Eve everything, except the fruit of one tree. He gave them only one little test of obedience. They could have lived without the fruit from that tree. It wasn't necessary for life. It was a little thing. God preferred the offering of Abel's lamb over Cain's fruit. It was a little thing. Surely Cain could have agreed with God and preferred the sacrifice of the Lamb, too. Why did Cain get angry about what pleased God? Surely Cain could have spared himself a great deal of trouble by simply agreeing with—or at least submitting to—God's preference. But he didn't. He rejected God's plan, got angry and succumbed to sin.

To the woman God said, your husband "shall rule over you" (Genesis 3:16). Paul wrote, "Wives, submit to your own husbands, as to the Lord" (Ephesians 5:22). But he also commanded that the husbands love their wives and submit to Christ. Husbands are charged to be faithful channels of God's authority over their wives and families.

People tend to go wrong when they think that wives are supposed to evaluate the effectiveness of their husband's faithfulness. Is the wife anywhere charged with the responsibility to insure that her husband is accurately or adequately performing his headship responsibilities? Is that not the job of a supervisor, one who has authority over another? The wife is not to act like a supervisor over her husband. Is anyone charged with such responsibility? Yes, the elders of the church are so charged. Husbands are to be in submission to the elders of their church. Furthermore, that kind of submission should be no more and no less than submission to Christ through Scripture. Submission to Christ requires submission to His ordained representatives. Any break in the order of authority and submission that God has ordained through Scripture produces sin and trouble.

Thus, when church elders themselves fail to live in submission to Christ, or husbands fail to live in submission to church elders, or wives fail to live in submission to their husbands, then God's order of authority for church and family, and ultimately for the world, breaks down and sin fills the authority vacuum. To correct the problem each party must fulfill his or her own responsibility—not someone else's, but his or her own. Each person must be faithful to the order of authority that God has given him or her. We cannot solve anyone else's problems or fix their failures, but we can and must deal with our own. Each Christian must live under his or her own God-given authorities, whoever they may be. Furthermore, Scripture calls for more than mere obedience, it calls each Christian to honor his or her "head." "Render therefore to all their due: taxes to whom taxes are due, customs to whom customs, fear to whom fear, honor to whom honor" (Romans 13:7).

> *"Now I praise you, brethren, that you remember me in all things and keep the traditions just as I delivered them to you. But I want you to know that the head of every man is Christ, the head of woman is man, and the head of Christ is God. Every man praying or prophesying, having his head covered, dishonors his head. But every woman who prays or prophesies with her head uncovered dishonors her head"* —1 Corinthians 11:2-5

HEAD COVERINGS

We cannot deal with the issue of authority without also dealing with head coverings. What are head coverings really about? How are we to understand Scripture in this matter? Is it important?

Examination of the issue reveals several things. First of all, it is not *my* (nor anyone's) responsibility to dictate the wearing of hats by anyone else. It is not even my place as a husband to dictate the practice to my own wife! Rather, Scripture says that the proper wearing of head coverings is a symbolic way to bestow honor upon our "head." It is not written to men so that they can insure that their wives wear head coverings. It is written directly to women, and that is significant.

Thus, women are to bestow honor upon their husbands by wearing head coverings during worship, and men bestow honor upon Christ by not wearing them during worship. In this way women witness to the world that they are willingly living under the authority of their husbands, and men witness to the world that they are willingly living under the authority of Christ.

Paul said, "Judge among yourselves. Is it proper for a woman to pray to God with her head uncovered?" (1 Corinthians 11:13). Here Paul tells us that this decision is a personal decision and must not be coerced. Honor cannot be coerced. If I honor the Lord, then I will do my best to love and obey Him, not because He commands it, but because I honestly desire to please Him. God's people are not coerced into obedience, rather, they love being obedient—in the little things as well as in the big. Love and honor cannot be commanded, but only freely given. Yet, God commands us to love and honor Him.

Secondly, Christians have traditionally conformed to Paul's teaching about head coverings for worship over the centuries. The only exception to this practice appears to be the majority of Christian women during the last century. Women wore hats to church even through the 1950s. Thus, the rise of the women's liberation movement (earlier it was called *women's suffrage*) and the rejection of head coverings for women in worship appear to correspond to one another. The Women's Liberation Movement got women out from under the wearing of head coverings, and out from under the authority of their husbands, and out from under biblical authority.

Thirdly, no one questions the biblical injunctions regarding head coverings as they are applied to men. Christian men have always removed their hats for worship, and continue to do so. And what is more, men appear to have done it cross culturally over the centuries. Only in relationship to women is the issue of head coverings ever questioned.

Fourthly, the plain reading of 1 Corinthians 11: 2-5 clearly indicates that men should uncover their heads for prayer and worship and women should cover theirs. Furthermore, this practice is not limited to any particular culture, but is cross-cultural. The matter of head coverings has survived from the Old Testament to the New. Thus, it is not limited to particular Christians of any particular nation, but is transcultural.

Fifthly, the decision about head coverings in worship belongs to God's Holy Spirit. So, study the Scripture yourself, and judge for yourself what you will do. As a Christian, of course, we are to make such decisions on the basis of Scripture, with Christian history as an aid.

Do you willingly accept God's authority? Or do you reject it?

No Other

And God spoke all these words, saying, I am the LORD your God, who has brought you out of the land of Egypt, out of the house of bondage. You shall have no other gods before Me.   —*Exodus 20:1-3*

Notice that God's First Commandment is premised upon God's grace. God identifies Himself as "the Lord *your* God" (Exodus20:1—italics added). Notice that God has already identified Himself as the owner or highest authority for a particular group of people, His people. Who these people are will be a topic of continuing conversation because it is crucial that we understand exactly who God's people are. Not all people have the same spiritual Father. Speaking to some, Jesus said, "You are of the Devil as father, and the lusts of your father you will do" (John 8:44). God's people, on the other hand, are the people to whom God has directed His commandments, with their accompanying promises of blessings or cursings (Deuteronomy 28).

The only real question that needs to be answered in this regard is, am *I* a child of God? Are *you* a child of God? Do God's commandments apply to *you* and to *me*? Each person must answer this question. In many respects it is the most fundamental question of the Bible and of human existence because it is a watershed question. If people answer *yes*, then they will understand God's Word to apply to them personally, and if they answer *no*, they will feel free to ignore it. The point that is made here is that God Himself recognized and asserted His special care and salvation over certain people, while others were left in their sins. Or we could say that some people receive God's gift of grace and some don't.

In addition, God claimed credit for bringing His people "out of the land of Egypt," which He also describes as "the house of bondage" (Exodus 20:2). The Exodus event has always been understood by Israel —and the rest of the world as well—as Israel's release from slavery and bondage by a foreign power. Thus, by God's grace alone Israel was freed from bondage and slavery. Before God gave His law (the Ten Commandments), He brought Israel out of bondage. By doing so He saved Israel *to* (and *for*) Himself. By His grace and mercy alone He asserted His sovereignty by saving and protecting His people so they could be used for His own purpose. Consequently, grace preceded law in the Old Testament.

GRACE PRECEDES LAW

We could take the argument back another step by observing that God created the earth and as a function of His grace alone put Adam and Eve in it. Creation itself was the result of God's grace. The point is that grace precedes law both historically and existentially. The Ten Commandments were then given to a people who were saved by grace from bondage and slavery. God's law was given as a way of life that would be free from bondage and slavery. Israel was not freed from one kind of bondage to be put into another. Rather, Israel was freed from bondage in order to live in freedom under God. However, Israel's freedom was never the freedom to do whatever she wanted, but was always the freedom to live in obedience to God, to God's law, God's way.

While God freed Israel from bondage and slavery, the very First Commandment that God gave to the newly freed Israel was, from a purely human perspective, a limitation upon their newly granted freedom. They were forbidden to worship other gods. From God's perspective, of course, this was not a limitation at all. Rather, the only real human freedom is freedom in Christ. Freedom under God is the only real freedom there is, everything else is bondage and slavery to sin. The other gods are not real, so worshiping them means enslavement to human ignorance and superstition—sin.

Again, man (the species) was never completely and entirely free to do whatever he wanted. God calls that kind of freedom *sin*. Rather, man's freedom, like his bondage, has always been derived from another. That is, God's people have always lived in obedience to a higher authority. In his freedom man is subject to God, and in his bondage and captivity, he is subject to sin and Satan. Man cannot live apart from a moral code, and that code will be either biblical or not biblical, either godly or demonic. Absolute freedom is not man's prerogative but God's alone.

This first principle of God's law (the First Commandment) is not just the foundation of law and social order, but is the first principle of God's Word and God's way of life from beginning to end. Everywhere this first principle of the law—the preeminence of God—is woven into every square inch of the fabric of a genuine relationship to the Lord. For instance, the *Shama*, proclaims God's preeminence.

> *"Hear, O Israel: The* Lord *our God, the* Lord *is one. You shall love the* Lord *your God with all your heart and with all your soul and with all your might. And these words that I command you today shall be on your heart. You shall teach them diligently to your children, and shall talk of them when you sit in your house, and when you walk by the way, and when you lie down, and when you rise. You shall bind them as a sign on your hand, and they shall be as frontlets between your eyes. You shall write them on the doorposts of your house and on your gates.* —Deuteronomy 6:4-9

Again, notice that the mere reception of God's Word reveals that God is the giver, the provider of grace and mercy. The mere act of speaking to man at all was an act of God's grace.

WILLING OBEDIENCE

In addition, not only does Scripture command "And you shall love the Lord your God with all your heart and with all your soul and with all your might" (Deuteronomy 6:4), but it insists that God's words, God's command "shall be in your heart." What does it mean to have something in your heart? It means to commit it to memory, as when we hide God's Word in our hearts. It also indicates our greatest desire or highest value. Thus, God commands that He alone be our greatest desire, our highest value. You can force people to do something, but you can't force anyone to *want* to do it. A person's desires are not under the control of someone else. Yet, God commands that His people love and desire Him above everything else.

Does God command what is impossible? No. But God does command what is out of the reach of man's ability alone. In fact, all of God's commands are beyond the ability of man alone to obey them. But they are not impossible. Rather, God's commands are intended to demonstrate the inability of man to accomplish what God demands. God shows us our weakness and depravity in order to lead us to reliance and dependence upon Him. He demands what only He can accomplish. Thus, He demands that His people depend entirely upon Him for salvation and for life. God's commands are quite possible, but only as we depend upon Him to accomplish them in us through the power of the Holy Spirit. Thus, the whole of God's law is a function of God's grace. The law depends upon grace. The law is built upon God's grace. And what is even more important, the law is the outworking of God's grace.

Another way to say it is that our obedience to the law constitutes our sanctification, our growth and maturity in the Spirit. The process of sanctification necessarily involves obedience to God's law. Christians grow and mature spiritually by practicing obedience to God's law. Which of God's laws? All of them. Not all of them at once, of course. But all of God's laws apply to the sanctification of God's people.

Christians are saved from the ultimate consequence of sin by the grace of God, who has established His law and the primary means of living out God's grace in peace and harmony. Christ has saved His people from damnation by freeing them from the consequences of sin. Having been freed from the consequences of sin, then, they are free to practice obedience to God's law to the best of their ability without the fear of the ultimate consequence of failure—damnation. We are freed *from* sin, and freed *for* obedience.

God's grace produces sanctification—obedience to God's law—in the lives of believers. Obedience to God's law is a fruit of the Spirit, a fruit of God's grace in the lives of believers. And that is precisely what people don't like to hear because it implicates them in the matter of obedience to God's law. Even people who think they are Christians don't like to hear this because it means that real spirituality, real spiritual maturity cannot happen apart from obedience to God's law. And it cannot be faked. Because God is the only one who can bring anyone into obedience to His law, no one can fake it. The issue of biblical obedience forces people to see whether their own spirituality is genuine.

Legalists And Libertarians

Isn't obedience to the law the same as legalism? No. Legalism uses obedience in order to earn or merit salvation. Those who think that they are saved or can be saved by obedience to Scripture are both mistaken and legalistic, no matter how well or poorly they are able to conform to Scripture because their intent is to use obedience to gain salvation. That is works-righteousness.

However, actual recipients of God's grace do in fact engage the process of sanctification by becoming increasingly obedient to God's Word. But as they grow in spiritual maturity through increased obedience, they do not become legalists simply because they conform more and more to God's Word. Legalism is not simply obedience to God's Word. Legalists are those who try to use obedience as a way or method to merit salvation. But all of God's people are called to grow in their obedience to God's Word.

However, mere growth in obedience does not make people legalists. God commands His people in every age and time to have no other gods before Him. God's people value God above all else. God's people grow in obedience to God's Word. However, genuine conformity to God's Word is not a mark of legalism, but of faithfulness.

The difficulty regarding the distinction between those who are genuinely faithful to the Lord and those who are trying to earn salvation by pretending conformity to God's Word is that the difference between them has to do with their hearts, their intentions, and their relationship with the Lord. The Lord knows the difference, we don't. We know it in ourselves, but we don't and can't know about other people, not perfectly. Knowing the difference is much more difficult for us as human beings. We are not privy to the inner workings of other people's hearts. But those who know the Lord truly, know whether their *own* hearts have been broken on the Rock of salvation or not.

Legalists are forever trying to impose God's Word upon other people—and it doesn't work because those who don't love the Lord won't listen, and those who really love the Lord don't need someone to impose God's Word upon them. Those who love the Lord actually want to please Him through obedience to His Word in everything they think and do.

Liberals, on the other hand, are forever denying the importance of obedience to God's Word—and that doesn't work either. Those who really love the Lord will not deny the importance of obedience to God's Word because they actually want to please the Lord through obedience to His Word in everything they think and do.

Thus, it will behoove us not to err on the side of legalism nor on the side of liberalism, but to simply love the Lord and desire to please Him through obedience to His word in everything we think and do—particularly as it relates to Christ's church and to the fellowship of His people.

ONE LAW

*And the L*ORD *said to Moses and Aaron, This is the ordinance of the Passover. No stranger shall eat of it. But every man's servant that is bought for silver, when you have circumcised him, then he shall eat of it. A foreigner and a hired servant shall not eat of it. It shall be eaten in one house. You shall not carry any of the flesh out of the house. Neither shall you break a bone of it. All the congregation of Israel shall keep it. And when a stranger shall stay with you, and desires to keep the Passover to the L*ORD*, let all his males be circumcised, and then let him come near and keep it. And he shall be as one that is born in the land. And no uncircumcised person shall eat of it. There shall be one law to the native, and to the visitor that stays among you. So all the sons of Israel did. Even as the L*ORD *commanded Moses and Aaron, so they did. And it happened the very same day, that the L*ORD *brought the sons of Israel out of the land of Egypt by their armies.*   —*Exodus 12:43-51*

What is the proper relationship for a New Testament Christian to have with God's Law? One simple-minded answer may be that God gave one law for the Israelites in the Old Testament and Jesus gave a new law for Christians in the New Testament. Many people subscribe to this simple but false answer. This answer is often based upon Romans 10:4, "For Christ is the end of the law for righteousness for everyone who believes."

People mistakenly think that this means that Jesus put an end to the law, that the Lord does not expect Christians to obey His law, that the reign of the law is over because Christ came to free His people from it. The Greek word translated as *end* is *telos*, which means achievement, fulfillment, or completed purpose. It doesn't mean that Jesus ended all application of the law to man, but that Jesus Christ Himself was the fulfillment or completed purpose of the law.

In fact, the Christian mission is not to bring people into a relationship with Christ, but to apply the Word of God—first to ourselves and our families, and only then to extend that application to the world. We are forever getting the cart before the horse. People want to share their faith before they themselves have assimilated it into their own lives.

Others attribute this mistaken understanding to Colossians 2:13-14, "And you, being dead in your sins and the uncircumcision of your flesh, He has made alive together with Him, having forgiven you all trespasses, blotting out the handwriting of ordinances that was against us, which was contrary to us, and has taken it out of the way, nailing it to the cross." Again, people want to think that these verses mean that the relationship between God's law and the Christian was broken or ended by Christ, but that is a misreading of this verse. God's law did not *end* with Christ but was *fulfilled* by Christ. Christ is the end of the law in the sense that He is the final part, piece or element of the law. Christ is the final revelation that makes God's law both possible and meaningful.

Paul meant that Christians do not practice the law in order to achieve or receive salvation. Rather, Christians practice the law because they can do so without fear of the ultimate consequences of failure. Christians are free to practice God's law without fear of damnation, even if they don't do it perfectly. The requirements that existed prior to Christ's fulfillment of the law no longer apply to those who are in Christ. Why not? Because Christ has fulfilled them. He has satisfied the demands or requirements of the law for His people. That does not mean that Christians are free to ignore the law, but that Christians are freed from the requirement to perfectly fulfill the law themselves in order to attain salvation. Christ fulfilled the law and the requirements for salvation for (on behalf of) His people. That is the good news of the gospel. The good news is not what we do or what we can do, but what Christ has already done.

Biblical Unity

Large numbers of Christians have gone astray because of confusion about this matter of the relationship between Christians and God's law. It is certainly true that Christ altered that relationship for His people, but He did not end it or break it. Rather, Christians are now related to God's law through Christ. But that does not excuse them from practicing God's law. God's law is not only eternal, but it is the foundation for biblical unity. The unity that Christ prayed for (John 17:21, Ephesians 4:3-5), is the unity of living under the same Lord, the same law, the law of God.

The confusion goes back to the Old Testament misunderstanding about God's chosen people (Deuteronomy 7:6). Israel was never intended to be a simple, biological, inheritable blood-line issuing from *Shem* (Genesis 9:26). While the Old Testament nation of Israel has always played a special role in God's salvation plan, the Semitic blood line was never understood in Scripture to represent or to be the fulfillment or completion of God's salvation plan. That role was always reserved for Jesus Christ.

This is a great confusion today in that people don't know what to do with the modern state of Israel. Do the biblical prophecies concern the modern state of Israel in a special or unique way, apart from the church of Jesus Christ? No, the Israel of God is the Church of Jesus Christ, and modern Jews may be part of that church, just as anyone may be, according to God's grace.

How do we know that? Because Paul tells us so everywhere in his epistles. But in addition, the nation of Israel was destroyed in A.D. 70 by Rome. Rome sacked the city of Jerusalem, destroyed the Temple, and scattered the people of Israel. Israel was destroyed for her faithlessness, and her refusal to recognize Christ as the Messiah. Consequently, the history of Christianity, the history of the New Testament, is a history without a nation of Israel since A.D. 70.

God's Israel

There was no nation of Israel until 1948. After World War II thousands of Jews who had fought against Hitler in several national armies could not, for various reasons, return to their homes. Many Jews had lost everything. They had no homes, nowhere to return to. The world was faced with a significant Jewish refugee problem. So, the Allied Powers redrew the map of the Middle East and included a new nation. They called it Israel. But from A.D. 70 to 1948 there was no nation of Israel.

Does that mean that the nation of Israel today has the same relationship to the Lord God as did the Old Testament nation of Israel? Not at all. The Israel after 1948 was created by man. There is no necessary connection between them. In fact, they are quite different in many respects. In particular the Old Testament Israel was a theocracy, the modern state of Israel is not. And this is a serious difference.

The point of this diversion is only that God has always dealt with His people according to one law or one body of law, His law, biblical law. The law is an immense subject, but the point is that all people are subject to God's law—everywhere and at all times. The world belongs to God. He created it and everything in it. It is like saying that everyone is always subject to the laws of nature because the laws of nature are always subject to God. No one is exempt, not even Jesus

Christ. And if Jesus was not exempt from it, neither are we!

The Lord said to Moses and Aaron, "There shall be one law to the native, and to the visitor that stays among you" (Exodus 12:49). Shortly after God revealed the Ten Commandments to Moses, He told Moses—and through Moses all of God's people—that His law, the Ten Commandments, would apply to both native born, those who were born Jews. and to strangers, non-Jewish people who lived with them. In other words, everyone—Jew and Gentile—was/is subject to God's law. There would not be two laws, one for Jews and one for everybody else. No! The Lord is the God of integrity and fairness.

Similarly, today there should not be one law for Americans and another for Congressmen.[1] There should not be one law for the rich and another for the poor. Everyone should be treated the same under the law. Everyone should have equal access to the law and to the means to defend themselves. God said it then, and it is still true in spite of the fact that it is not practiced today.

To make sure that Israel understood that God was serious about this He repeated Himself in Leviticus 24:22, "One judgment shall be for you whether an alien or a native; for I am the LORD your God." To make sure that Israel understood that this was not a temporary arrangement, He said in Numbers 15:15, "One ordinance for you of the congregation and also for the stranger that resides with you, an ordinance forever in your generations. As you are, so the stranger shall be before the LORD." This was to be in force forever. God reiterated the permanence of His law by speaking through the prophet Malachi (3:6), the last of the Old Testament prophets, " For I am the LORD, I change not." As Christians we understand the eternal nature of God as well. God does not change, neither His character nor His purpose. The writer of Hebrews (13:8) wrote, "Jesus Christ the same yesterday and today and forever."

GOD'S GRACE

But what about God's grace? Doesn't the fact of God's free gift of salvation for all His people by the unmerited grace of God nullify the law for believers? Does not Paul sum up the third chapter of Romans, "Do we then make the Law void through faith? Let it not be! But we establish the Law" (Romans 3:31)? Indeed he does. Does Paul contradict himself? Not at all.

It is very important that we understand Paul's teaching about Christ and the law because it shows us how Christians are rightly related to the law. As Paul said, Christians are justified by faith without

---

1   "Should Congress Be Above the Law?" November 2, 1993, Updating Backgrounder
No. 965, The Heritage Foundation, Washington, D.C.

regard for any sins that they have committed. Christians are justified without reference to God's law. That is why we say that Scripture teaches that salvation is an unmerited gift from God. Receiving the gift of salvation does not depend upon nor require anything from us or on our part—no certain behavior, no particular obedience, not even any regard for God. Salvation is from God alone. He decides it. He initiates it. He completes it.

But the whole of salvation is composed of more than justification. Notice that Paul said that "a man is justified by faith *without the works of the law.*" (Romans 3:28—italics added). God is the author and provider of both justification and sanctification, and justification is accomplished by God apart from His law.

However, sanctification—growth in holiness, which is also a gift of grace from the hand of God—occurs through the increasing faithfulness or obedience to God's law. Sanctification, also a gift of grace, results from the gift of the Holy Spirit, who provides the means or ability to keep God's law. The point is not that God provides the ability or means of sanctification (although He does), but that sanctification is accomplished by adherence to God's law.

OBEDIENCE

Yet, Christians are not charged to maintain every Old Testament practice. And here lies the difficulty. Exactly what are we as Christians to obey, and what are we free to ignore? First of all, we can ignore nothing because "All Scripture is God-breathed, and is profitable for doctrine, for reproof, for correction, for instruction in righteousness" (2 Timothy 3:16). We must learn from it all, but that doesn't mean that we must do exactly as the saints of the Old Testament did. Christ has come! And some things have changed because of it.

Surely, we are not to maintain the Old Testament system of Temple sacrifices! Christ is our perfect sacrifice (Hebrews 7:27). Of course, we are not, because Jesus Christ our High Priest offered Himself as the atoning sacrifice for the sins of His people (Hebrews 8). "Nor by the blood of goats and calves, but by His own blood He entered once for all into the Holy of Holies, having obtained eternal redemption for us" (Hebrews 9:12). His sacrifice has satisfied God for all time.

Yet it is not completely true that Christ ended all ceremonial law or practices. Ceremony continues to be important, but the nature and practice of various ceremonies has changed. Our New Testament ceremonies do not *anticipate* Christ, they *celebrate* Him. Our communion service is as much a ceremony as was the sacrifice of lambs and bulls in the Old Testament. But because Christ has come, because His blood has been shed, because propitiation has been made, the nature and practice of the ceremony has changed to point to the fact of His manifestation in the life of Jesus Christ.

Yet, it should be abundantly clear that all of the Ten Commandments remain in force. The Lord clarified the intent and purpose of the Ten Commandments, which brought to light some of the earlier over-reactions or narrow-minded, legalistic understandings and practices related to them. For instance, He altered some Sabbath practices that were misinterpreted by the Pharisees. We will talk about those when we get to the Fourth Commandment. For now we are concerned with the First Commandment. Clearly, Jesus honored and kept the First Commandment and taught His people to do the same.

A lawyer came to Jesus and asked, "Which is the first commandment of all?" Jesus answered him, "The first of all the commandments is: 'Hear, O Israel, the LORD our God, the LORD is one. And you shall love the LORD your God with all your heart, with all your soul, with all your mind, and with all your strength.' This is the first commandment" (Mark 12:28-30). Jesus quoted the *Shema*.

When Jesus called it the "first commandment," He didn't simply mean that it was the first in a list. The Greek word translated *first* is *protos*, which means first in rank, influence, and honor. Think of the word *prototype*, which is the first of a kind, an original. The first commandment generates all the rest. The others are dependent upon the first as a house is dependent upon a foundation, as a child is dependent upon his father. God's oneness, God's unity is the foundation of His law. Thus, it behooves us to understand God's oneness and unity thoroughly and to regard it with the highest honor. The oneness and unity of the Lord are functions of His law. God's law is the source of biblical unity.

PRACTICAL APPLICATION

But how can we do this? What are some practical ways we can implement the First Commandment in our lives? Since the Lord is one and His law is one, we must recognize its unity. First, we must maintain unity among believers by understanding the usefulness and extent of God's law. And secondly, we must maintain unity between the Old Testament and the New, particularly regarding the nature and practice of God's law. The unity of God's nature and law imply unity between the Testaments and unity among believers, even between Old Testament and New Testament believers. Traditionally this unity was expressed as the Judeo-Christian heritage of the Western world. But it must be understood to mean believers who anticipated Christ and those who celebrate Jesus Chirst.

Original sin is the prototype violation of God's first commandment. Adam's sin amounted to a disregard for God's Word, God's law. Original sin always manifests itself as the substitution of man's authority for God's. Adam's sin amounted to following his own authority, his own advice, rather than God's. Adam valued human thinking, human evaluation, the desires of his own heart, above God's Word. He did what was right in his own eyes.

Scripture is adamant about the sinfulness of this practice, and deals with it extensively. For example: Judges 17:6, Judges 21:25, Isaiah 5:21, Proverbs 3:7, 12:15; 14:12; 16:25; 21:2; 26:12; 26:16; 30:12, Psalm 36:2, Luke 11:39, Luke 16:15, 2 Timothy 3:5, Titus 1:16, Galatians 6:3, James 1:22, 1 John 1:8. This list is only representative, not comprehensive. The briefest consideration of Scripture as a whole must admit to this important truth.

What can we do to practice the First Commandment? We must acknowledge that we are all subject to God and to God's authority. To be subject to God means to be subject to God's various authorities—personal conscience, family, church, and state.

First, God's people recognize that they are subject to these authorities whether or not they agree with them. Only when these lesser authorities require us to deny God's ultimate authority can we refuse obedience, and submit ourselves to God's Word directly.

Secondly, God's people actually desire to live in accordance with God's Word in everything. Thus, obedience is not imposed from without, but is desired from within. No one has to force Christians to be obedient. They do it because they want to do it.

Thirdly, God's people demonstrate to the watching world their own commitment and submission to God's Word and God's authority. Christians are not embarrassed by their obedience, but are comforted by it.

Covenant Symbols

And when Abram was ninety-nine years old, the Lord appeared to Abram and said to him, I am the Almighty God! Walk before Me and be perfect. And I will make My covenant between Me and you, and will multiply you exceedingly. And Abram fell on his face. And God talked with him, saying, As for Me, behold! My covenant is with you, and you shall be a father of many nations. Neither shall your name any more be called Abram, but your name shall be Abraham. For I have made you a father of many nations. And I will make you exceedingly fruitful, greatly so, and I will make nations of you, and kings shall come out of you. And I will establish My covenant between Me and you and your seed after you in their generations for an everlasting covenant, to be a God to you and to your seed after you. And I will give the land to you in which you are a stranger, and to your seed after you, all the land of Canaan, for an everlasting possession. And I will be their God. And God said to Abraham, And you shall keep My covenant, you and your seed after you in their generations. This is My covenant, which you shall keep, between Me and you and your seed after you. Every male child among you shall be circumcised. And you shall circumcise the flesh of your foreskin. And it shall be a token of the covenant between Me and you. And a son of eight days shall be circumcised among you, every male child in your generations; he that is born in the house, or bought with silver of any stranger who is not of your seed. He that is born in your house, and he that is bought with your silver, must be circumcised. And my covenant shall be in your flesh for an everlasting covenant. And the uncircumcised male child whose flesh of his foreskin is not circumcised, that soul shall be cut off from his people; he has broken My covenant. —Genesis 17:1-14

And the Lord said, Shall I hide from Abraham the thing which I do, And Abraham shall surely become a great and mighty nation, and

all the persons of the earth shall be blessed in him? For I know him,
that he will command his sons and his house after him, and they
shall keep the way of the LORD, to do justice and judgment, that the
LORD may bring upon Abraham that which He has spoken of him.
                                              —Genesis 18:17-19

God's law is the basis for God's covenant. A covenant is an alliance or a pledge made between two or more parties. God's covenant is His pledge to mankind that He will relate to us through the means of His law, through Scripture. The giving or establishment of that law was an act of great grace and mercy.

God's first gift of grace was creation itself, which not only included the creation of humanity, but creation itself was a gift for humanity. God's second gift of grace was God's law or the enscripturation of His Word. God's Word provides the only means for life as God intended it to be lived, the only way that human life can be sustained in peace. God's third gift of grace was Jesus Christ and His cross work, the provision for a salvation that cannot be earned or otherwise obtained apart from the atonement of Jesus Christ. These three gifts—creation, Word, and Christ—provide the fullness of God's grace. Three gifts of grace for the salvation of God's people.

Covenant Membership

God's law, God's Word is His covenant. His covenant, His pledge or promise to His people is not just an extension of His Word, but it is His Word itself—the Bible, Old Testament and New. God's Word is His provision for His people. The law was given as a schoolmaster for His people, to bring them to see their own depravity and their need for Christ. And Christ was given as a propitiation for sin, so that God's people can—by the grace and mercy provided by the atonement of Jesus Christ—practice and actually live on the basis of God's Word, God's law. God's Law brings us to the grace of Christ, who provides us with the means to practice God's law. Christians are not freed *from* obedience to God's law, but are freed *for* obedience to God's law. We are freed from sin and delusion by the atonement of Christ and through the power of the Holy Spirit.

Thus, those who practice the First Commandment, who have no other gods before the Lord, are members of God's covenant. Of course we know that people cannot obey God as a way to be included in His covenant. Rather, by the grace of Jesus Christ and the power of the Holy Spirit, covenant inclusion is a function of God's grace through faith. We do not and cannot make ourselves members of God's covenant. Rather, God makes people members of His covenant by the bestowal of His Holy Spirit. God regenerates sinners, who are then made members of His covenant.

The order is significant. People are not Christian because they say they are. People are Christian because God says they are. Just as babies are not the agents of their own birth, so those born-again in Christ are not the agents of their own rebirth. When we say that God is our Father, we mean that He caused our new birth. We did not cause ourselves to be reborn. The order is significant because it points to the fact that God is the Father of the twice-born. I am not my own spiritual father, but God is my spiritual father.

COVENANT SYMBOLS

The symbolism of God's covenant is important for the same reasons. The Old Testament symbols of the covenant were circumcision and the Passover meal. The New Testament symbols of God's covenant are baptism and communion.

Genesis 17:9-14 provided the institution of circumcision as a sign or symbol of the covenant. Circumcision was the first symbolic act of obedience required by God. It is the paradigm or model for the relationship between God and man, particularly regarding this issue of biblical or moral obedience. Thus, the practice of circumcision reveals the relationship between God and man in a foundational way.

Only males were circumcised because God deals directly with males through the biblical principle of headship. God's covenantal government is representational government, so representational elements were embedded into the symbols of the covenant. God is the ultimate authority in the world, and operates by means of His own authority. He brings males directly under His authority (probably because human masculinity tends to be dominant) and then sets men up as heads of households so that they can exercise God's authority in the family. This establishes God's authority throughout the fabric of human society through the exercise of man's authority in submission to God, and does so in a representational manner. All biblical authority is in some regard representational and, thus, is authority in submission to God and to His representatives.

People today are up in arms because Scripture calls women to submit to their husbands (Ephesians 5:22). But Scripture also calls men to submit to Christ (James 4:7). When this biblical relationship works as it is supposed to, the greater burden is not upon women, but upon men. It's not that women do not have a legitimate beef with their self-centered husbands. They do! Rather, the problem is rooted in the selfish ungodliness of their husbands. Women cannot be properly submitted to their husbands—submitted as Scripture commands—

unless and until their husbands are properly submitted to Christ. So, where a wife is in rebellion the husband is at fault (1 Timothy 2:14).

The point is that the sign of the covenant was given only to men who were also given to the Lord in submission to the practice of circumcision, which was to serve as a sign of covenant obedience. And, interestingly, this sign of God's covenant was both a public sign and a private sign. While the act of circumcision was ceremoniously done by a Rabbi and announced to the whole community, you could not observe the sign of the covenant as a circumcised man walked down the street. Rather, the only people who would have any experience or proof of the sign would be the man's parents (who inflicted it upon him) and his wife. Thus, this sign of the covenant was a family matter.

But not merely a family matter. Circumcision was authorized by the church, performed by the Rabbi and witnessed by representative elders, friends and extended family. Thus, circumcision was also a church matter.

Was circumcision a sign of the covenant for women as well as for men? Yes, it was. Did women participate in this sign of the covenant? Yes, they did, by the power and principle of representation. Representational authority is a key concept in Scripture. Yet, the covenant sign or symbol that God gave (circumcision) was not directly observed by the public. Rather, the public would only indirectly see the effects of God's covenant in a family through the family's obedience to God's authority, and to God's representative, the husband/father. This was God's covenant headship model given to His people through the institution of circumcision. Circumcision was the sign of the covenant "worn" by the head of the family. Circumcision symbolized and established God's order for the family and for the church.

PASSOVER

There are several other interesting things to notice about circumcision. It was a prerequisite for keeping the Passover (Exodus 12:48-49). Only the circumcised were allowed to share or partake in the Passover celebration. In a similar way Christian baptism is a traditional prerequisite for receiving communion. Both circumcision and baptism are understood to be initiation rites or ceremonies. A person should be initiated prior to covenant participation.

Circumcision was the first step of obedience to God's law. Obedience not only required new converts to be circumcised themselves, but to circumcise their male children. Similarly, baptism is often the first step of obedience for Christians. And it is an obedience that is both personal and representational. Parents bring their children to be baptized before the child can make any choices, which then emphasizes the representational authority of the head of the household. In other words, infant baptism is in fact done on the basis of a free choice, but it is the choice of the head of the household not the infant. And because the child is under the authority of the head, and the authority is real, the decision applies to him or her. In addition, the earliest baptism practices seem to have followed the same covenantal practices regarding children (Acts 16:15; 1 Corinthians 1:16).

The Old Testament norm was infant circumcision, but some Old Testament Jews who were converted as adults were also circumcised as adults. Abraham was circumcised when he was ninety-nine-years-old (Genesis 17:24). However, the covenant institution of circumcision was designed to be performed upon male infants, eight days old (Genesis 17:12). Thus, the ordinary method of circumcision was infant circumcision. Why infants? First and foremost because that's what God commanded. It should be enough that God commanded it, but let's look at the symbolism involved.

Circumcision opposed paganism and the symbolism associated with paganism. All paganism is man-centered religion, whereas biblical religion is God-centered. How so? Only the biblical God is real. Pagan gods are not real. In addition, Pagan religious rites are initiated by man in order to influence God. Pagan ceremonies seek to gain God's favor by some personal or priestly merit. Whereas biblical rites (covenant signs) are initiated by God in order to influence man. Pagan ceremonies try to get God to act in some particular way, where biblical ceremonies sought to get men to act in some particular way—to obey God.

PAGANISM

Logically and legally, the initiating party has both authority and responsibility regarding the action called for by the initiating action. If I accuse someone in court, I am both authorized and responsible to prove the case. I can pursue the action or drop it. The party that initiates is in the driver's seat, so to speak. The other party can counter, etc., but their counter becomes a separate initiation of another action.

Thus, pagan people believe that they exercise religious authority because they are able to initiate various religious practices that will influence God in some way. Today, some ostensibly Christian practices have taken on this pagan character. It is not difficult from this perspective and understanding to see the pagan character of Pelegianism and Arminianism. So, when Christian practices and ceremonies center on man, on human activity, they reveal themselves to be more pagan than biblical.

On the other hand, God's people believe that God exercises religious authority because He has initiated various actions and/or religious practices in order to influence us, to make His people obedient by giving them the desire and the strength to actually conform their lives to God's commands. Circumcision is the chief symbol of this biblical belief. How so?

PASSIVE BEFORE THE LORD

The infant child is completely unable to initiate or perform the rite of circumcision for himself. He is brought to it and it is performed upon him completely apart from any will or desire on his part. Circumcision is God's doing from start to finish. God commanded it and then inflicts it upon helpless infants.

Did the Old Testament teach that every circumcised Jew would be saved? That every circumcised child would prove faithful to God's covenant? No, there was not a necessary relationship between circumcision and faithfulness. Circumcised Jews could and can fail in their covenant responsibilities just as anyone can fail to live in obedience to God's Word. But the practice of circumcision meant that circumcised children would be raised in covenant homes by parents who were making an effort to be faithful, and to teach faithfulness to their children. Their parents' faithfulness would, then, provide an additional help and incentive to those children to be faithful themselves.

Did the Old Testament teach an ethnic salvation, that being Jewish was somehow equivalent to being saved? Not at all. Notice Genesis 17:5, "Neither shall your name any more be called Abram, but your name shall be Abraham. For I have made you a father of many nations." The Hebrew word translated *nations* is *gowy*, which means *people*, but includes heathen and Gentile people. There are two possible interpretations here and both are correct. First, it meant that Abraham would be the father of some nations that he would not sire. And second, it meant that not all of the physical seed of Abraham would be faithful to God, though all were to be circumcised.

Notice also Genesis 17:12, "And a son of eight days shall be circumcised among you, every male child in your generations; he that is born in the house, or bought with silver of any stranger who is not of your seed." God commanded circumcision of all males in covenant homes, not just the genetic Jewish males. Every male residing in a covenant home was to be circumcised. Thus, the sign of the covenant from the beginning was not to be a practice limited to ethnic Jews, but was inclusive of all who participated in God's family covenant.

GUARANTEE

Another misunderstanding teaches that circumcision guaranteed faithfulness. Scripture never teaches that circumcision amounted to some sort of magical rite that guaranteed covenant faithfulness. Circumcision was to be a sign or symbol that served the growth of spiritual fruit. Deuteronomy 10:16 taught, "Therefore, circumcise the foreskin of your heart, and be no longer stiff-necked." The Old Testament taught the importance of circumcision of the heart, where circumcision of the heart amounts to holiness, conformity to God's precepts, but mostly it taught that the heart must desire God. Similarly Deuteronomy 30:6, "And the LORD your God will circumcise your heart and the heart of your seed, to love the LORD your God with all your heart and with all your soul, so that you may live."

Circumcision was a sign and symbol of covenant headship, of family headship because family headship is the first level of covenant headship. It was never intended to be understood as a magical rite, but always symbolized God's initiative in salvation, God's power in sanctification, and man's personal, moral responsibility. Circumcision doesn't confer ability. It symbolizes God's sovereign grace and man's personal responsibility.

Is the Old Testament circumcision rite still in effect? Should Christians practice circumcision? What about circumcision of the heart? Scripture itself teaches that circumcision is a sign of God's eternal covenant and since God's covenant is eternal, so is its sign. What does it symbolize about God's eternal covenant? Circumcision symbolizes God's grace through His initiating action of drawing people into covenant relationship with Him. And it symbolizes family headship—representative authority. Biblical headship can also be called representative family government. The head of the family represents his family before God, and God before his family.

This is not a minor concern since Christ represents His people before God, and represents God before His people as well. Christ's atonement for His people on the cross requires the reality of representative government before God and man. So, family headship, male headship—because God defined it that way—is essential to a proper understanding and effective application of the atonement of Christ.

But before we get carried away, we must realize that the ceremony of circumcision was itself representational. It represented what Scripture calls the circumcision of the heart. That is to say that the point of ceremonial circumcision was never the simple removal of a flap of skin, but pointed to the more important reality of heart circumcision, or a "new heart" (Ezekiel 36:26). In the New Testament the reality is always more important than the symbol or the ceremony.

Representative Government

Why am I talking about circumcision? What has this got to do with us as Christians? The biblical principle that drives the practice of circumcision is the principle of covenant headship, or representative government, which provides the organizational structure for biblical families. The same organizational structure—representative government—applies to the church because the church is an extension of the family. It is based upon the same organizational structure. Thus, as God's people gather, that organizational structure provides the basis, the pattern, for the gathering. The failure to get this right effects everything else that Christians think and do.

If our families do not function according to God's plan—covenant headship or representative government, then our fellowship or church will not be able to function according to God's plan either. So, we need to return to the biblical model for families, so that we can return to the biblical model for churches. These two institutions are linked together in Scripture.

Ground zero for all of this to happen according to Scripture is love and respect. God's people must love and respect God. We must trust God to do what is right, as we must love and trust Jesus, and love and trust our own parents and one another. The love of the brethren is the fuel of the church. We must love and trust God and one another enough that we can come together, so that we can be fully honest in one another's company. We need to love and trust Jesus Christ and one another so that we can honestly repent, confess our failings, receive forgiveness, and press on, "toward the mark for the prize of the high calling of God in Christ Jesus" (Philippians 3:14).

MERCY TO THOUSANDS

You shall not make to yourselves any graven image, or any likeness of anything that is in the heavens above, or that is in the earth beneath, or that is in the water under the earth. You shall not bow yourself down to them, nor serve them. For I the LORD your God am a jealous God, visiting the iniquity of the fathers upon the sons to the third and fourth generation of those that hate me, and showing mercy to thousands of those that love Me and keep My commandments.   *—Exodus 20:4-6*

In Exodus 19 God reminds His people that He brought them out of bondage in Egypt. We remember that as Moses negotiated with Pharaoh to let God's people go, he reported that God wanted them to go out in order to worship the Lord. The purpose of that worship would climax in God's giving of the Ten Commandments. God was taking His people from bondage to human sin, from ignorance of God to personal and corporate freedom through obedience to God. This passage from bondage to freedom, from sin to righteousness, is not what it seems to be to most people. Unregenerate people view everything inside-out, upside-down, and backwards from the way that God sees things.[2] The passage from bondage to sin to freedom in Christ provides a great example of the reversal of values that accompanies regeneration.

What God calls bondage to sin, most people call freedom. People are indeed free to do what they want, or to do what they choose. But whenever people do this their choices (and actions) are based upon their own values, their own judgments, their own thoughts and ideas. Thus, their choices and actions are limited or determined by their personal values and abilities. People act according to their own

---

2   See *Arsy Varsy—Reclaiming The Gospel in First Corinthians,* by Phillip A. Ross, Pilgrim Platform, Marietta, Ohio, 2008.

thoughts, values, feelings, ideas, abilities, etc. And this kind of behavior is called freedom because, it is believed, that this behavior is not coerced by anyone else. When people do what *they themselves* choose to do they call it freedom.

However, such freedom does not and cannot consider the wisdom of God. Sin has closed people off from being able to understand God's wisdom. So, God calls it sin because it does not even consider His thoughts and ideas, much less obey them. And how could a mere human being take an omnipotent God's thoughts and ideas into consideration? It is absurd to think that people can assess or evaluate God's thoughts and ideas! People can't even adequately or correctly think God's thoughts, much less evaluate them.

Nonetheless, God loves His people and has set out a way of life that will provide them with everything they need. At the heart of this way of life are God's laws, the Ten Commandments. Apart from Christ, God's law is a schoolmaster that demonstrates our personal (human) inability to properly consider or obey God's law. The schoolmaster drives God's people to see their need for Christ and to depend upon Him. But once people see their need for Christ and begin to depend upon Him, He invariably sends His people back to God's law to live by it. While apart from Christ obedience to God's law is impossible, in Christ obedience to God's law becomes the very desire of the regenerated heart. While perfect obedience is impossible, actual—though faulty—obedience in Christ is effectively engaged. One of the ways people can assess their own faithfulness is to see if they actually want to please God in all they do.

JEALOUS

Faithfulness to God is very much like faithfulness to one's spouse, and that is probably why Scripture describes God as "jealous" (Exodus 20:5). At the same time, God's jealousy is not like human jealousy in that God is not fearful or wary of being supplanted by another. While that does indeed happen, people do forsake God for idols, God is not fearful or worried about it. Nor is God apprehensive about losing the affection of His people, or His position as the only real God. God is not resentful or bitter when people abandon Him, though Scripture tells us that His anger can wax hot against those who deny Him. God is not envious of the false gods who supplant Him in the hearts of many people. God's jealousy, like His anger, is righteous.

So, what is God's jealousy about? Like a jealous husband, God is vigilant about guarding something valuable. His relationship with His people is of infinite value and eternal duration. It is important. And if it is going to work, that relationship must be kept in purity. Like a marriage, it must be kept inviolate in order to function as it was designed. Thus, God is intolerant of disloyalty or infidelity in His relationship with people.

The purpose of God's jealousy is to keep that relationship pure, right, whole, complete—not on God's part, but on ours. God's jealousy serves His glory. His purpose is to establish His rule and reign on the earth. God is truth and righteousness, so His rule and reign are the rule and reign of truth and righteousness. God forbids idolatry because idolatry undermines truth and righteousness.

Exodus 20:5 tells us that God "visit(s) the iniquity of the fathers on the sons to the third and fourth generations of those who hate (Him)." In plain English this means that the punishment of one generation can carry over into other generations in one of two ways. God may either delay punishment for generations or continue it for generations. Scripture is saying two things here: First, that God's mercy may continue to indulge the iniquity of the fathers for as long as three or four generations before God manifests His judgment. It may take three of four generations of sinning before God brings judgment to its fulfillment. Second, the judgment or punishment that God brings may last as long as three or four generations. Both of these ideas are conveyed in this verse.

The judgment that God brings is related to the iniquity of the fathers. But what is iniquity? What are these sins of the fathers that bring God's judgment? The word *iniquity* means unevenness, inequality, injustice. It means inequitable, not level or equal. Iniquity is the lack of justice or righteousness. And it is "the iniquity of the fathers" that is of concern.

Most generally it means *sin*. This verse means that sometimes God does not thoroughly punish people for their sins during this life. God sometimes—even often—reserves the fullness of His judgment and punishment for the life to come, that is, through damnation in hell.

Again, God is saying two things here. First, while punishment for sin begins in this life, the fullness of that punishment is executed in hell for sinners. And second, sometimes the consequences of the sins of one generation in this world continue in this world into future generations. The punishment for sin (or the mess that sin causes in this world) can have effects that continue for generations.

Thus, the children of sinners can reap the fruit of their parents' sin. The scope and magnitude of God's judgment can be multi-generational. God is big and does things in a big way. This multi-generational aspect of God's judgment ought to bring the fear of God to anyone who loves their children. To think that my children will experience the effects of my decisions is an awesome thought. It should help us all to see that, while we are individuals, we are not really independent from one another.

Nonetheless, God's judgment is reserved for those who hate Him (Exodus 20:5). The multi-generational aspects of God's judgment are reserved for those generations who continue to hate the Lord. Notice that punishment continues for those who hate the Lord. Everything that is said about God visiting the iniquity of the fathers on the children to the third and fourth generations has to do with those who hate the Lord.

MERCY

However, as horrendous as the thought of God's judgment extending for generations is, it pales in comparison to the graciousness of God's mercy. Verse 6 tells us that God's mercy is granted "to thousands, to those who love Me and keep My commandments." Thousands of what? Thousands of generations! God's mercy will continue for thousands of generations as long as people love Him and keep His commandments. A thousand generations! How long is a thousand generations? If a generation is 25 or 30 years, then a thousand generations is 25,000 or 30,000 years! That's practically eternity compared to the length of a human life, and is about five times as long as all of recorded human history to date. It's a long time.

Notice that here in the midst of giving the Second Commandment to Moses, God poured out His grace and love and mercy for His people. His love and mercy are so great He cannot contain them. While the Second Commandment forbids idolatry, the reason that God gives it is because He wants to extend His grace and mercy to this lost and sinful world—to thousands of generations! The very giving of God's Law is an act of grace and mercy to His people.

God's law is a gift of grace. God's law is not opposed to grace. It is itself a gift of grace, given to assist the salvation of God's people. People are not saved by the law, they are saved for the law. Thus, God's commandment against idolatry and superstition is a gift of grace. It is an act of mercy and is intended to provide grace and mercy for God's people for thousands of generations.

It has been said that God's law is a schoolmaster who's purpose is to bring people to Christ. And that is true. But we must not think that God's law is merely a truant officer, one who goes out and rounds up delinquent students and brings them to class. A schoolmaster is primarily a teacher. God's law is a teacher. The purpose of God's law is to teach. Likewise, the responsibility of students is to obey the teacher, to study and learn the lessons. A schoolmaster has the obligation to teach, and the students have the responsibility to learn.

There is much confusion regarding the idea that Christ frees His people from the law. According to Galatians 3:13, God's people have been freed from the curse of the law and at the same time given a genuine love of the law. In Christ we are free from the consequences of failure to perfectly obey the law. Christ Himself has received those consequences in our stead. But that fact does not end our relationship with God's law. Rather, it frees us to practice the law as best as we are able, without the fear of failure, without the fear of receiving the consequences of failure. We are free in Christ to do our best to obey God's law, knowing that our obedience will be imperfect and unworthy. But we know that Christ's atonement has supplied what we cannot supply. The point is that in Christ we are not free from responsibility to obey God's law, we are free to give it our best shot, knowing that if we truly do our best, it will be sufficient when covered by the blood of Christ.

Is it possible to live without idolatry and superstition? It is, but only in Christ. Only when we respond to the Lord's "knock" and give ourselves fully to Jesus Christ. Only when we submit to God's Word as best we can, as best we understand it, in the willingness to continue to grow in it and to increasingly submit ourselves to it as our understanding of it increases. Yet, such submission is not simply a duty. It is not engaged in order to attain salvation, but only in response to a salvation already given, a salvation already completed by the atonement of Christ on the cross.

The law chases us into the arms of Christ, and Christ returns us to God's law, not simply to the obligations of the law, but now in Christ we find ourselves in love with God's law. With the assurance of Christ's salvation we can practice God's law without the fear of failure. How do you know if you truly love the law? How do you know if you truly love Jesus Christ? How do you know if you truly love anyone or anything? You just do.

And so does God!

VANITY

You shall not take the name of the Lᴏʀᴅ your God in vain. For the Lᴏʀᴅ will not hold him guiltless that takes His name in vain.
—*Exodus 20:7*

Don't take (or use) the Lord's name in vain. The Hebrew word for vain is *shav*, and it is rightly translated as *vain*. But what does it mean to take or use something in vain, to use or do something vainly, or in vanity?

To do something in vanity means that nothing comes of it. *Vain* means empty or false. It means to be without substance or effect. To use something unproductively is to use it vainly. To lie or tell a falsehood is to act of vanity. Yet, there is another sense of the word *vain*. Because it has to do with emptiness and falsehood, it also carries the sense of desolate. To use the Lord's name in vain is to desolate or desecrate it. Desolation of what belongs to the Lord is a sacrilege, a violation of something sacred.

But why is misuse of God's name such a terrible thing? God's name is holy because God is holy. To be holy is to be dedicated or set apart for special service. When God revealed His name to Moses at the Burning Bush, God said that His name is "I ᴀᴍ ᴛʜᴀᴛ I ᴀᴍ. And He said, So you shall say to the sons of Israel, I ᴀᴍ has sent me to you." (Exodus 3:14). When we pray the Lord's Prayer we say, "Our Father who is in heaven, Hallowed be Your name" (Matthew 6:9). *Hallowed* means holy. It suggests that God's name is sanctified, set apart for special service. Paul tells us that "whoever shall call on the name of the Lᴏʀᴅ will be saved" (Romans 10:13). And Peter said "there is no other name under Heaven given among men by which we must be saved" (Acts 4:12). John said that "as many as received Him, He gave to them the authority to become the children of God, to those who believe on His name" (John 1:12).

The name of Jesus Christ has the power to save! To name some-thing is to tell what it is. To name it falsely or wrongly is to misunder-stand it or to not know it. And to fail to know the Lord Jesus Christ by name is to miss salvation itself.

Leviticus 24: 10-16 tells of a man who was stoned to death for cursing and blaspheming the name of the Lord. The man was the son of an Israelite woman, whose father was an Egyptian. The guilty man is never described as an Israelite himself. In addition, it says that he struggled with an Israelite.

It would seem that we have a blended household here. The woman was a believer and her husband was not. Their son then struggled with another believer and cursed and blasphemed God in the struggle. Who knows exactly why it happened or what was going on. Scripture doesn't tell us what the nature of the struggle was. Apparently it didn't matter. The important point is that this son of an Israelite woman was punished because of a violation of God's law.

That in itself is quite interesting. It suggests that God's law applied to all covenant children, whether or not those children actually confessed or believed or obeyed the Lord themselves. But the point to see here is that violation against the Third Commandment was punish-able by death, and that penalty was enforced in this instance.

Was it fair? The law said that the action was punishable by death. The boy violated the law, and the death penalty ensued. Is it fair to enforce the law? If you want to argue about the nature of the law, take it up with God. It's His law. We may argue with this or that law today. I mean state or civil laws. But regardless of how we feel about them, their enforcement is not a matter of individual decision. The law may seem unfair, but its enforcement is not illegal. God's law, on the other hand, is always just (fair) for two reasons: First, because God's char-acter is just, and second, because God defines justice.

SWEAR FALSELY

Leviticus 19:12 tells us "not (to) swear by (God's) name falsely." Here the word *swear* does not mean curse, it means to take an oath. Does it mean that Christians should take no oaths or vows at all using the name of God? Or that Christians should take no false or vain oaths or vows, that people should not make promises that they do not intend or cannot keep? Obviously, people should keep their promises, particu-larly in reference to God, but no less should people make false promises to one another. But what about vows, oaths, and/or promises made to God or that invoke God's name?

The Third Commandment is about taking "the name of the Lord your God in vain" (Exodus 20:7). The Hebrew word for name is *shem*, and refers to one's character or reputation. Again, the Hebrew word for vain is *shav* and means emptiness, vanity, or falsehood. Thus, the Third Commandment forbids blasphemy and/or desecration of God's name.

Cursing and cussing are definitely forbidden. But there is more to this commandment than that. It is also forbidden to vow to God or take an oath to God or make a promise to the Lord that is not kept. Any and all vows or promises that are made must be honored and kept. Failure to do so constitutes a violation of the Third Commandment. God forbids false promises, empty promises, promises that come to nothing. God forbids broken promises.

But does that mean that God forbids making any promises, any vows, any oaths at all? Psalm 50:14 reads, "Offer to God thanksgiving; and pay your vows to the Most High;" Psalm 56:12 (KVJ) reads, "Vows made to You are binding upon me, O God; I will render praises to You." Psalm 76:11 instructs God's people to "Vow, and pay to the LORD your God; let all that are around Him bring presents to the Fearful One."

In the light of these verses, how are we to understand Matthew 5:33-37, "Again, you have heard that it has been said to the ancients, You shall not swear falsely, but you shall perform your oaths to the Lord. But I say to you, Do not swear at all! Not by Heaven, because it is God's throne; not by the earth, for it is the footstool of His feet; not by Jerusalem, because it is the city of the great King; nor shall you swear by your head, because you cannot make one hair white or black. But let your word be, Yes, yes; No, no. For whatever is more than these comes from evil"? These verses occur in Jesus' Sermon on the mount, where Jesus explains, refines and brings the law to bear upon human intentions as well as actions.

Jesus acknowledged the Old Testament laws about false swearing (using God's name vainly), but tells His people not to swear at all, not to make any special promises. Why?

The argument goes like this: if I tell you that I am promising to do something particular, I'm suggesting that the promise I am making is more trustworthy than my usual words. Promising something is like saying, "This time I mean it. This time my words are more true than they usually are." Jesus wants all of our words to always be true, so there are no lapses in integrity that require some special promises or oaths. Make all of your words true and trustworthy so when you say *yes* you mean *yes* and when you say *no* you mean *no*. James 5:12 repeats the same admonition.

Does this mean, for instance, that Christians should not take the oath in a court of law when they take the stand? Certainly it means that among Christians such an oath should not be necessary. The courts require swearing to tell the whole truth and nothing but the truth so that they can prosecute you with perjury if you lie while under oath. They believe that the threat of prosecution helps to insure your truthfulness. Should a Christian take such an oath?

While my understanding of this issue is incomplete, and is not set in stone, it seems to me that Scripture does not necessarily preclude taking such an oath. By taking such an oath in a court of law, a person is promising to tell the truth, which is exactly what Jesus wants us to do all the time. But Jesus wants us, not to limit our truth telling to the times that we are under oath, but to always tell the truth. If people did that, oaths would be of no use.

In addition, it seems that Jesus' admonition here is not specifically directed toward court situations, but is directed at life generally. Thus, the Third Commandment is about honoring God, who is truth, by honoring truthfulness in everything that we say and do. It's about honoring God's integrity, and our own.

This is the commandment that Jesus was accused of breaking by the Sanhedrin. "The Jews answered Him, saying, We do not stone you for a good work, but for blasphemy, and because you, being a man, make yourself God" (John 10:33). Jesus applied the name of God to Himself, and the Jews thought that He did that in error, that it was not true. Thus, being a false use of God's name, it constituted a violation of the Third Commandment. If Jesus were not God incarnate, their accusation would be true. But because Jesus is God incarnate, their accusation was false. Nonetheless, they believed that Jesus was liable to the death penalty, as was the boy previously discussed.

The application of the Third Commandment requires honesty and integrity of all Christians in all situations. We must be honest in all our dealings with other people. And most important, honesty and integrity are required in our relationship with Jesus Christ. In other words, it is a violation of this commandment for someone to say that he or she is a Christian if it is not true, or if he doesn't really believe it himself. To claim salvation in Jesus Christ falsely or wrongly is a violation of the Third Commandment. To mistakenly claim Christ because of a misunderstanding of the gospel also violates the Third Commandment. The only claim to salvation in Christ that does not violate this commandment is a true claim, which is only to say that salvation in Christ is true only when it is true. Conversely, it is wrong to say it is true when it isn't.

Understanding this rightly raises the stakes regarding one's personal profession of faith, as well it should! The use of God's name is not a neutral act. The use of God's name necessarily moves people toward salvation or damnation. There is no middle ground, no middle or neutral position. To use God's name falsely or wrongly is to invoke your own damnation. Similarly, to use God's name truly is to invoke

God's salvation.

Thus, by the power of the Holy Spirit, who makes it true, Christians are able to claim salvation in Christ. If God has drawn you to believe that Jesus is the Christ, and brought you to confession of your sins and reception of forgiveness, you will be saved. (Romans 10:9). And there can be no doubt about it!

Lord, make it so.

Resting In God

*Remember the Sabbath day, to keep it holy. Six days you shall labor
and do all your work. But the seventh day is the Sabbath of the* Lord
*your God. You shall not do any work, you nor your son, nor your
daughter, your manservant, nor your maidservant, nor your cattle,
nor your stranger within your gates. For in six days the* Lord *made
the heavens and the earth, the sea, and all that is in them, and
rested the seventh day. Therefore the* Lord *blessed the Sabbath day,
and sanctified it.*   —*Exodus 20:8-11*

God's Sabbath Commandment has provided a host of issues,
struggles, and difficulties for modern Christians. Perhaps it has
done the same for God's people in all ages, I don't know. But I
do know of some of the modern concerns.

Scripture itself speaks a lot about the Sabbath. The Sabbath is so
important to the Lord that punishment for its violation is death, "You
shall keep the Sabbath therefore, for it is holy to you. Everyone that
defiles it shall surely be put to death. For whoever does any work in it,
that soul shall be cut off from among his people" (Exodus 31:14).
Violation of this commandment was punishable by death according to
the Old Testament. That makes it pretty serious, more serious than
people today think it is.

It would be difficult to determine whether the Lord said more
about the Sabbath (Fourth Commandment) or idolatry (Third
Commandment). But in the Decalog itself, four verses were given to
the Fourth Commandment and three to the Third. Unlike the other
Commandments, the first statement of this commandment (v. 8), is
positive, "Remember the Sabbath day, to keep it holy." Not until verse
10 do we find the usual negative prohibition, "You shall not do any
work...."

The fact that most of the Ten Commandments are negative prohibitions is very interesting. God is quite explicit about what He forbids,

but says much less about what He permits. There is no question about what is forbidden, but it almost seems as if He wants us to be actively engaged in the determination of what pleases Him. Obedience to the prohibitions is required, but if we want to go the second mile to please the Lord we have to work at it. Obedience is a duty, but pleasing the Lord is above and beyond the call of duty. To love the Lord is to please Him.

The question always comes up about working to maintain essential services during the Sabbath. Are people who work essential service jobs allowed to work on the Sabbath? Of course, they are. Matthew 12:11 provides justification for Sabbath rescue services. Jesus healed on the Sabbath, justifying medical services (Luke 6:6). Much of Jesus' ministry corrected the Pharisees' narrow understanding of the Sabbath. However, if we find ourselves trying to justify various kinds of work on the Sabbath, we are likely in violation of the Sabbath principle already. The principle of the Sabbath is to focus on God, not on ourselves.

The purpose of the Sabbath is to punctuate our regular work schedule with godly concerns. That requires the cessation of those things that regularly distract us, and work is usually a primary distraction. Thus, we are to cease working. That much is easy. But the Lord takes it another step, "You shall not do any work, you nor your son, nor your daughter, your manservant, nor your maidservant, nor your cattle, nor your stranger within your gates" (v. 10). It appears that the entire household is to cease its ordinary activities. But what does that mean? What sort of activity is forbidden?

If we look at who is commanded not to work, we can better determine what not to do. First, we can say that whatever regular job you have, it means don't do it on the Sabbath. To begin to list exceptions to Sabbath prohibitions, as tempting as that is, only sets us off in the wrong direction. Our concern is not to justify the exceptions, but to do all we can to maintain the rule. At the same time, we must understand that there are exceptions, but God's command intends to keep the exceptions to an absolute minimum.

The command not to work includes children, so we can say that regular school activities should cease. The command includes male and female servants, so we can say that domestic service should cease—no cooking, cleaning, yard work, house work, etc. When you think about it, the Sabbath Commandment seems to be directed at households. If nobody goes to work, then everybody stays home. The whole family is off, together at the same time. Everybody is home.

The Westminster Confession added recreation to the list of things not to do. The Westminster Confession calls for a "holy rest, all the day, from (our) own works, words, and thoughts about (our) worldly employments, and recreations" (Chapter 21). There is a sense in which the writers of the Westminster Confession were right to add a prohibition against recreations. They were trying to deal with people who were distracted from the Sabbath by their recreational activities. They noticed that people were not working on the Sabbath, but were flocking to the country or the river or the beach or the ski slopes, or shopping, etc. Many people work hard at their recreations. The point of the Sabbath is to set a block of time aside for the Lord—worship, Bible study, fellowship, and service. Recreation, like work, is a distraction.

It is possible to fail in our Sabbath responsibilities because we are distracted by recreational activities. However, the problem is not recreation per se, but faithlessness and irresponsibility. People can be distracted by anything. It is not the distraction that is the problem, but the faithlessness. The prohibition against Sabbath recreation is a man-made addition to Scripture. Sure, recreation can get out of hand, but family oriented recreation and games on the Sabbath are entirely appropriate—in the Lord. Sabbath recreation is not prohibited in Scripture when it occurs within the context of genuine fellowship.

The issue of Sabbath recreation brings up an important point. How do we know what we are supposed to do on the Sabbath? God told us what *not* to do, but did He tell us what to do? God has everyone off work and at home. Is the Sabbath supposed to be a house full of people sitting around staring at each other, doing nothing? No, the Sabbath is to be a positive, helpful, restful, refreshing day. So, what are we supposed to do on the Sabbath?

BE REFRESHED

Paul wrote to the Romans in the hope of visiting them. He was excited by the prospect and wrote, "so that I may come to you with joy by the will of God, and may be refreshed with you" (Romans 15:32). This sort of refreshment is the purpose of the Sabbath. The Sabbath is not to be the mere cessation of work related activity, but is to provide an alternative activity that brings refreshment and restoration. That does not exclude, for instance, taking a nap. Naps are refreshing. But we are not limited to naps either. It includes being refreshed in the Lord in an active, positive sense.

The Greek word that Paul used in Romans was *sunanapauomai*. It is the only use of this particular word in the Bible. Interestingly, the word has covenant overtones because it suggests the kind of rest and refreshment enjoyed by husband and wife when they nap together. The Greek word to describe God's Sabbath rest in Hebrews 4:4 was *katapauo*. The common root of these words is *pauo*, which means *pause*.

Sabbath obedience is about the pause that refreshes, to borrow a commercial slogan.

SIGNIFICANT ORDER

The Decalog is divided into two tablets. The first four Commandments pertain to our relationship with God, the last six to our relationships with each other. The Ten Commandments are also given in a particular order. The order is neither random nor insignificant. There is a purpose to it that serves our sanctification, our growth in the Lord.

The first three Commandments require that we abandon everything false about our relationship to the Lord. Because there are no other gods, we shall have no other gods before the Lord. Nor shall we make graven images. We don't know what God looks like, so any attempt to imagine or replicate God will be necessarily false. Neither shall we use God's name falsely or vainly.

The Sabbath Commandment is quite different from the preceding three. It does not begin with a negative prohibition, but a call to remember the order of creation. It contains a negative prohibition, but doesn't begin there. It begins with an appeal to memory, to creation, and to history.

Verse 11 tells us that "in six days the LORD made the heavens and the earth, the sea, and all that is in them, and rested the seventh day. Therefore the LORD blessed the Sabbath day, and sanctified it." The concluding sentence tells us that the reason the Lord sanctified the Sabbath was because it was the day that He rested, the day He paused to reflect on creation, the day He was refreshed by His reflection. All of creation was good. In fact, it was very good!

God's Sabbath is an invitation to rest, to rejoice, to be refreshed, in God's creation by honoring God's sovereignty over time itself. God's Sabbath is about time. It's about the sanctification of time, about separating a certain period of time from the rest of time. It's really about God's sovereignty over time, over our personal time. Our time is not our own. Anyone who works knows that. But God's Sabbath tells us that even our so-called free time is not our own. Rather, our free time, willingly given to God in Sabbath obedience, is the climax or purpose of creation. Sabbath obedience, not just willingly but joyfully given, is the greatest expression of God's glory that mere human beings can offer.

Yet, we find the Old Testament filled with accusations against Israel for breaking God's Sabbath. Not once, not twice, but over and over people have ignored God's Sabbath to their detriment. We find ourselves living in a time of Sabbath ignorance. People don't know about the Sabbath, and don't care about it. It is widely ignored today.

While mindless, faithless observance of the Sabbath can accomplish nothing but to rouse God's wrath and anger, faithful observance of the Sabbath is a mark of faithfulness that not so much brings revival as it is itself the essence or activity of revival. The Lord spoke through Isaiah 58:13-14:

> *If you turn your foot because of the Sabbath, from doing what you please on My holy days, and call the Sabbath a delight, the holy of the Lord, honorable; and shall honor Him, not doing your own ways, nor finding your own pleasure, nor speaking your own words, then you shall delight yourself in the Lord; and I will cause you to ride on the high places of the earth, and feed yourself with the inheritance of Jacob your father. For the mouth of the Lord has spoken.*

Here we can see that Sabbath obedience requires a turning of the heart from its own pleasures, thoughts, and concerns, to the service of God's pleasures, thoughts, and concerns. Genuine Sabbath obedience is a work of love for God and a mark of regeneration. Because the dead cannot regenerate themselves, Sabbath obedience is only possible for the redeemed. Only in Christ can Sabbath rest be enjoyed, or even seriously engaged. Yet, God chastises both the unregenerate and the regenerate for disobedience. God does indeed chastise His own people for their own good, for the growth and development of their faith. While worldly people simply will not conform to the Sabbath command—or to any other, there is no excuse for Christians not to obey the Lord.

Christ died in part to provide Sabbath rest for His people. The Sabbath is not incidental or coincidental to the purpose of creation. Rather, the engagement of the Sabbath is the purpose of both creation and salvation. Sabbath rest and refreshment is part of the glory of creation. It was for God Himself, and it is for God's creature, man.

How is your Sabbath rest?

Resting In Christ

*Remember the Sabbath day, to keep it holy. Six days you shall labor
and do all your work. But the seventh day is the Sabbath of the LORD
your God. You shall not do any work, you nor your son, nor your
daughter, your manservant, nor your maidservant, nor your cattle,
nor your stranger within your gates. For in six days the LORD made
the heavens and the earth, the sea, and all that is in them, and
rested the seventh day. Therefore the LORD blessed the Sabbath day,
and sanctified it.*   *—Exodus 20:8-11*

No human being is completely free. Every individual is bound
by his own limitations—intelligence, ability, opportunity, etc.
We are also bound by law—God's law, human law, social
customs, etc. No one has absolute or complete freedom. All human
freedom is limited freedom. God's Sabbath Command constitutes the
principle of human freedom under God.

Freedom under God's law provides the greatest freedom possible.
God's law provides greater freedom than human law, and greater
freedom than social customs. As odd as it sounds to non-Christians,
obedience to God's Word is perfect freedom. Conversely, to fail to live
in obedience to God's Word is to limit human freedom for both Christians and non-Christians. And, of course, the fullness of obedience to
God is only possible when it arises out of genuine love, love that is
freely given, love voluntarily expressed, obedience voluntarily given.

Obedience to the Sabbath Commandment provides freedom from
tyranny and freedom from bondage to work. There are two kinds of
tyranny. Tyranny can be imposed upon one person by another, or it
can be imposed upon a person by himself. The first kind is what we
usually think of as tyranny, one person forcing his will upon another.
But the second kind is actually more common.

SELF-BOUND

People are often bound by their own oppressive will. Most people think of freedom as doing what they want. But when we understand that the thoughts and desires of people are themselves sinful, it is easier to understand this kind of freedom as the Lord does, as bondage to sin.

Perhaps some definitions are in order. Something is oppressive when it cannot be escaped. Sinners are unable of themselves to do anything other than what they want. They have no thoughts other than their own thoughts, no desires other than their own desires. Thus, they are limited—bound—by their own thoughts and desires. They cannot get beyond them. Everyone is in this condition, not just some people, not just certain people, "for all have sinned and come short of the glory of God" (Romans 3:23). Sinners are self-concerned, self-centered, and sometimes self-obsessed.

People think that freedom is being able to do whatever they want. The highest expression of this kind of freedom is to be able to do anything and everything that you want to do. People call this *freedom*, but God calls it *sin*. From God's perspective, such a view limits human beings to their own selfish and sinful desires. God wants much more than this for us. God wants us to accomplish His will for our own sakes. He wants us to want to do His will in our lives. And His will is much more expansive and encompassing than our own. It is our own will that is narrow-minded. God's will is actually much more broad-minded that most people believe.

Only by giving ourselves to God's will can we escape the limitations we impose upon ourselves, that limit us to our own feeble wisdom and paltry abilities. Unregenerate sinners can see no other options than their own abilities and wisdom, or at best human abilities and human wisdom. Regenerate sinners can see that their own desires are flawed and sinful, and that only by the regenerating power of the Holy Spirit can people overcome our bondage to our own limited, selfish, and sinful desires. It is for the breaking of this bondage that the Sabbath Commandment has been given.

The Sabbath commandment calls God's people to rest. The verb *rest* has several meanings. The most common meaning is to cease from activity. But Sabbath rest means more than the mere cessation of work. To rest means to be refreshed, rejuvenated, and renewed as well. The primary Old Testament understanding of the Sabbath was a day of rest, not simply a day of corporate worship.

The pattern of weekly worship did not exist until it was introduced in the synagogues during the intertestamental period (200 B.C. to 200 A.D.). Old Testament worship was primarily family worship. Jews were required to make a pilgrimage to the temple once a year, but regular, weekly worship was incorporated in the family Sabbath. The New Testament church continued the synagogue pattern of weekly corporate worship (Hebrews 10:25), but this practice did not replace family worship. Rather, it augmented it. It became an additional responsibility. Because worship is not a burden but a joy, the additional responsibility of weekly corporate worship is not an additional burden, but an additional joy. If worship is good, more worship is better!

Reliance Upon

The word *rest* also means to depend or rely upon, i.e., the burden of proof *rests* upon the defense. The Sabbath is also a command to rest in God's authority, God's sovereignty, God's providence. To practice Sabbath rest is to proclaim the sovereignty of God, to proclaim that there is no authority above the Word of the Lord, no power greater than God. More than simply proclaiming it, the Sabbath is a call to rest in it, to place our trust and confidence in God's Word as the highest authority.

When God rescued Israel from slavery in Egypt, Israel was taken out of Pharaoh's authority and placed under God's authority. Pharaoh didn't want Israel going out to worship because God's demand for worship placed Israel outside of Pharaoh's authority or jurisdiction. Moses, however, honored the authority of God over the authority of Pharaoh. Pharaoh's resistance to let Israel go into the wilderness to worship was an issue of authority, and Pharaoh knew it.

God's authority is not always nor necessarily opposed to human authority or state authority. They are not in necessary opposition. But opposition can exist when secular or state authority forbids what God allows, or allows what God forbids. They are only in opposition when state authority opposes God's Word.

The Sabbath observance helps God's people celebrate and honor God's authority over every aspect of their lives by demonstrating God's sovereignty and human subordination to God's Word. Sabbath observation honors God's sovereignty.

The Pharisees continually attacked Jesus for breaking the Sabbath law. They didn't like the fact that His is disciples picked corn on the Sabbath (Luke 6:1), or that Jesus healed on the Sabbath (Luke 6:7). The Pharisees taught that both of these things broke the Sabbath law. The Sabbath law did indeed forbid gathering, as in harvesting and collecting firewood (Exodus 35:3, Numbers 15:32). But when it comes to healing on the Sabbath, we encounter something new from the Pharisees. Nothing in the Old Testament forbade Sabbath healing, unless healing is understood as a human work.

The purpose of the Sabbath—to rest in the Lord—can only be fulfilled in Jesus Christ. To rest in the Lord requires the forgiveness of sin, an atonement that is acceptable to God to repair the breach of sin originated by Adam in the garden. Until that breach is repaired there can be no rest in the Lord. Until the enmity between man and God is healed, rest in the Lord is impossible.

When Jesus healed on the Sabbath He demonstrated that the healing He brought to the world was the very purpose of the Sabbath. How could the purpose of the Sabbath be forbidden on the Sabbath? It couldn't. Jesus brought light and life to a world darkened by sin and death. The restoration of life, the resurrection of the dead, provided the means for Sabbath rest. The Sabbath in the light of Christ is a celebration of life. It's a celebration of new life in Christ.

The Old Testament Sabbath anticipated the coming of the Messiah, and the healing of enmity. All of the Old Testament looked forward to the coming of Christ. That anticipation or looking forward to something is sometimes called foreshadowing. The Old Testament sacrifices and ceremonies prepared God's people to receive and understand the great and necessary sacrifice of Jesus Christ on the cross (Colossians 2:17). But once the atoning sacrifice of Christ was made, the Old Testament sacrifices and ceremonies were put in their proper perspective, that of preparing God's people by anticipating the incarnation and atonement of Jesus Christ.

Once Christ came and offered His atoning sacrifice on the cross, it was inappropriate to look forward to Him as if He hadn't already come. In fact, to continue to anticipate the coming of Christ after the fact was to deny that He had actually come. It constitutes a denial of Christ's divinity. For these reasons the Lord made some changes to Sabbath practice. The Sabbath could no longer anticipate Christ. He had come! The anticipation was fulfilled.

Only the Lord Himself could make such changes, and in doing so He expressed two things about Himself. First, He asserted His authority as God to alter His law. Second, He demonstrated His love and concern for His people by reminding them that the "Sabbath was made for man, and not man for the Sabbath" (Mark 2:27). The Sabbath is a blessing to God's people, as is all of God's law. The purpose of God's law is not to punish, but to bless. The punishments are given in order to dissuade us from doing things that will hurt us. God's law points to love, happiness, fulfillment, and rest in the Lord. God's law is a gift of grace and mercy.

The fact that the Pharisees accused Jesus of breaking Sabbath law only served to demonstrate that the Pharisees themselves had taken God's law farther than Scripture warranted. Scripture forbade all work on the Sabbath, yet the priests worked on the Sabbath, demonstrating that the Sabbath law had some exemptions. The exception given to the priests allowed them to work for the cause of the Lord's salvation of His people. They continued to make sacrifices and perform ceremonies on the Sabbath. Jesus claimed that exemption for His disciples when they picked and ate corn on the Sabbath (Luke 6:4).

Saturday

Why don't Christians worship on Saturday? Doesn't the word *Sabbath* mean Saturday?

Yes, it does. First of all, our Julian calendar does not correspond with the ancient Jewish calendar. So, our Saturday is not equivalent to the ancient Jewish Sabbath. Secondly, the New Testament church gathered on Sunday because Sunday was the day that Jesus rose from the dead. Jesus' resurrection or regeneration was understood to be the fulfillment of the Sabbath purpose of healing the enmity between God and man so that God's people could rest in the Lord.

For Christians, Christ's resurrection and their own regeneration are the fulfillment of the Sabbath purpose, and are appropriately celebrated on Sunday, the day of the celebration of new life or resurrection in Christ. However, the ordinance against work did not simply transfer to the Christian Sabbath.

The first day of the week, Sunday, was a Roman work day during the First Century. Roman Christians who had jobs worked on Sunday. So, the church gathered in the evenings after work. The coming of Christ brought new meaning to the Sabbath. For First Century Christians it was not primarily a negative prohibition against work, but a positive celebration of new life in Christ. The essence of the Christian Sabbath is rest in Christ and growth in the knowledge of His salvation.

Thus, work on the Christian Sabbath is not strictly forbidden, but is discouraged as much as possible so that Christians can give the day to rest and the concerns of the Lord. If a person has to work, he can take his Sabbath rest another day. However, this should not be done lightly or casually because it usually means that he will miss the gathering of the saints for worship.

The purpose and function of the Sabbath has not changed, but has been fulfilled in Christ. Thus, the seriousness of the Old Testament prohibitions—the commitment to Sabbath obedience because of the fear of God—should be part of the New Testament Sabbath, except that New Testament obedience should issue from the love of Christ rather than the fear of God.

Sabbath obedience for Christians is a celebration of Christ's atonement and their own regeneration by the power of the Holy Spirit.

While Sabbath disregard cannot nullify Christ's atonement, it does call into question the regeneration of those who disregard it because the Sabbath should be an engagement of refreshment and joy.

How is your Sabbath observance?

Principles of Family Honor

Honor your father and your mother, so that your days may be long upon the land which the Lord your God gives you.   —Exodus 20:12

The command to honor father and mother is concerned with the offices of parenthood and the social structure of the family. The command is generalized in such a way as to refer to family roles rather than the particular individuals who inhabit those roles. The command is not simply aimed at particular individuals—not to *my* mom and dad or *yours*, but it sets forth the blueprint of the family itself. To honor mother and father is to recognize and respect the God-given structure and authority of the family itself.

Inheritance

There are four principles inherent in this command. The first principle regards the laws of inheritance. To a great extent we are what we have inherited from our parents—physically, mentally, and culturally. Our physical inheritance pertains to our bodies, our minds, and our wealth. Children inherit their parents' genes, their parent's values, and to a certain extent their parents' wealth and/or property.

Everything that God created reproduces according to its kind (Genesis 1:24). Man is no exception. There are variations within kind (or species) that are based upon the existing gene pool. But parents and children share much in common from a common gene pool. This is one aspect of our inheritance.

In addition, we inherit what our parents teach us about God, the world, and society. This is the cultural deposit of our inheritance. To respect our parents is to respect their wisdom about life. This does not mean that every set of parents is full of good and godly wisdom. They are not! Nonetheless, children generally absorb the values and traditions of their parents, whatever the values of the parents are. The

58

child of an alcoholic is more likely to be faced with the temptation of alcoholism. The child of an abuser is more likely to become an abuser. Similarly, the child of a born-again Christian is more likely to hear the gospel, and thus, come to the Lord himself. It is difficult to discern if these kinds of things come from genes or social behaviors. But it doesn't really matter because they are real either way.

We inherit physical characteristics, behavioral characteristics, and personal values from our parents. Again, that does not mean that every child of an alcoholic will become an alcoholic, nor that every child of a Christian will become a Christian. It only means that there is a tendency for children to be like their parents. This is true whether or not the children want to become like their parents. Much of it is beyond our control.

PROGRESS

The second principle acknowledges that human or social progress is rooted in history. History is the foundation of progress in the same way that science is the foundation of technology. Progress does not come from breaking with the past, but from honoring it, from building upon it. Social or cultural revolution, from God's perspective, impedes progress because it does not build upon history, but destroys it. It does not and cannot enhance genuine progress because revolution destroys the basis of God-given authority and inheritance that are required for social progress. Similarly, technology cannot be advanced by the repudiation of science. Technological advancement requires that science be honored and built upon, not dishonored and torn down.

The values and forces of revolution oppose the values and forces of progress. Revolution must destroy authority and inheritance to be successful. Revolution is fueled by impatience, greed, and selfishness, where progress in God's kingdom is fueled by patience, service and selflessness. The kingdom of God cannot be produced by revolution—personal, social, or cultural. Rather, the Kingdom of God honors history, builds upon cumulative inheritance, and respects law. The kingdom of God is a matter of obedience, not insubordination, a matter of inheritance, not imposition. The kingdom is timeless. It is neither old and dusty, nor new and fashionable. It is always applicable, relevant and appropriate.

Another aspect of this second principle pertains to ownership of property. The tradition of inheritance indicates that property ownership is a function of the family. Inheritance laws demonstrate that property belongs to families. The argument is simple. Even our current laws support the idea that property and wealth are first and foremost family matters. We see in our own society that the most successful families are able to keep property within their families, in spite of the obstacles of the legal system.

Reward

The third principle is that God rewards human behavior. "For the Son of man shall come in the glory of His Father with His angels, and then He shall reward each one according to his works" (Matthew 16:27). Earlier the Lord spoke through Jeremiah (17:10): "I the Lord search the heart, I try the reins, even to give to each man according to his ways, according to the fruit of his doings." Paul said that the Fifth Commandment "is the first commandment with a promise" (Ephesians 6:2). What is that promise? It is that God will reward the faithful, "that your days may be long upon the land which the Lord your God gives you" (Exodus 20:12). Psalm 62:12 declares, "Also to You, O Lord, belongs mercy; for You give to every man according to his work."

The family is the place that most human behavior is learned, so the family plays a very significant role in the justice that God metes out to His people. For the most part what we learn in our families stays with us all our lives—and beyond. Again, this does not mean that salvation can be learned or inherited from one's family. We cannot earn salvation for ourselves, nor can we learn ourselves into the Kingdom. Neither can we give it to our children. We can, however, make sure that our children learn the Bible and hear the gospel. They may accept it, or they may reject it. We don't have control over that. But we can teach the Bible and present the gospel. And we must!

Salvation is not the reward of doing good or of learning the right things. Salvation is not a reward for anything. "For by grace you are saved through faith, and that not of yourselves, it is the gift of God, not of works, lest anyone should boast" (Ephesians 2:8-9). Nor is the theme of salvation by grace alone unique to the New Testament. It is also found in the Old Testament.

> He led you through the great and terrible wilderness, with fiery serpents and scorpions and thirsty ground, where there was no water, who brought you forth water out of the rock of flint, who fed you in the wilderness with manna which your fathers did not know, so that He might humble you and so that He might prove you, to do you good in your latter end, and so that you might not say in your heart, My power and the might of my hand has gotten me this wealth. But you shall remember the Lord your God, for it is He who gives you power to get wealth, so that He may confirm His covenant which He has sworn to your fathers, as it is today.
> —Deuteronomy 8:15-18

PUNISHMENT

The fourth principle inherent in the Fifth Commandment applies to the inverse of the command. Dishonor of parents or disobedience of any of God's ordained authorities makes for the dishonoring of one's self and is an invitation to death. This principle results from the negative promises of God. "And it shall be, if you will not listen to the voice of the LORD your God, to observe and to do all His commandments and His statutes which I command you today, all these curses shall come on you and overtake you" (Deuteronomy 28:15).

Because God uses the word *if* here and elsewhere, it sometimes seems as if these promises are contingent, that they depend upon our ability to keep God's covenant. God says, *If* you obey you will receive blessings, and *if* you disobey you will receive cursings (Deuteronomy 28). Since salvation is God's greatest blessing, people often think that their salvation depends upon their ability to obey the Lord. That's almost right, but not quite.

Salvation and obedience are connected. But it is not that obedience brings salvation, but that salvation brings obedience. Salvation does not depend upon our ability to obey, but upon God's ability to keep His promises. When God keeps His promise to save His people, His people are enabled to keep their promises of obedience.

There is no contingency regarding salvation in Deuteronomy 28, nor any in the entire Bible. God said that those who receive His blessings *will* be saved, and those who receive His curses will not. God said, "I will be gracious to whom I will be gracious, and will have mercy on whom I will have mercy" (Exodus 33:19).

REBELLION

When Korah and others rebelled against Moses and Aaron, they accused them of taking "too much upon you, since all the congregation are holy, every one of them, and the LORD is among them. Why then do you lift yourselves up above the congregation of the LORD?" (Numbers 16:3). They thought that Moses and Aaron were making themselves too important among God's people. They wanted in on the leadership and the benefits they supposed came from biblical leadership. They presumed God's blessings for themselves (Deuteronomy 1:43).

Moses fell on his face when he heard the accusation because he knew it was blasphemy. "Even tomorrow the LORD will show who are His, and him who is holy, and will cause him to come near to Him; even him whom He has chosen, He will cause to come near to Him" (Numbers 16:3), he replied. In verse 7 Moses said, "And it shall be the man whom the LORD chooses, he shall be holy. You take too much upon you, sons of Levi!" Finally, God caused the earth to open and swallow

Korah and his men because of their sin of claiming the Lord's blessing for themselves.

Korah rebelled against God's decision to give Moses the authority to lead the people of Israel. Here we see this fourth principle in operation in the Old Testament. Moses was given God's authority to lead Israel. The rejection of God always means the rejection of God's authority, and the rejection of those whom God has given authority—husbands and fathers who have family authority, pastors and teachers who have church authority, leaders of the state who have governmental authority, and finally of God Himself who has ultimate spiritual authority. Because all authority has been ordained by God, the rejection or disregard of any authority amounts to the rejection of God Himself. It is no small matter, but is at the very heart of sin.

God gave all authority to Jesus Christ for the salvation of His people. That salvation includes the justification accomplished by Christ's death and God's calling. It includes sanctification, which is in part the gathering of His people in spiritual fellowship. And finally it culminates in glorification, the consummation of His people in heaven.

RESPECT

The command to honor your father and mother is the command to respect God-given authority wherever it is found. But the first place that every person finds it is in his own family. That is where it begins, and that is where the Lord wages the battle for authority. The family is the first place the Lord establishes His authority. To loose the battle there creates a cascade of ripple effects that have serious consequences throughout society.

FAMILY ORDER

Honor your father and your mother, so that your days may be long
upon the land which the Lord *your God gives you.*   —*Exodus 20:12*

S cripture commands that godly parents be honored. To honor
something is to hold it in due respect. Honor is an attitude, but
it also results in action and activity. Here it means that parents
be willingly obeyed. The action of parental honor means acquiescence
not merely to the commands and wishes of the parents themselves,
but to the biblical law they ideally uphold. To honor the law means
not only to hold it in high regard, but in a practical sense it means to
obey it.

The Fifth Commandment is, thus, the practical basis for God's
authority in the lives of His people. The Fifth Commandment is the
experiential foundation of all authority. The ultimate foundation of
God's authority is God's omnipotence. But the practical foundation of
His authority is parental obedience. If children fail to respect, honor,
defer to, and obey their parents, they will fail to respect, honor, defer
to, and obey God, and other social authorities.

The relationship between God and His people corresponds to the
relationship between parents and their children. At first, children
obey their parents out of fear of punishment. But as they grow, they
learn to love their parents and willingly defer to them on the basis of
that love. So it is with God's children. The family is the primary
teacher of authority, and as such, it is the foundation of all social
order. The family is the linchpin of social order. Its maintenance
secures social order, and its neglect or destruction destroys social
order.

PROMISE

The promise associated with the Fifth Commandment pertains to both personal and social longevity, "so that your days may be long upon the land which the LORD your God gives you" (Exodus 20:12). Notice that it is a promise pertaining to life in this world. The promise attached to the Fifth Commandment is not other-worldly, but this-worldly. It is about earth not heaven. Thus, it is practical, relevant and real.

But the promise is not just about obedience to the Fifth Commandment. If the Fifth Commandment is honored, then all of the other commandments will be honored as well because the parents are charged to teach their children the whole law. Leviticus 10:11 instructs God's people to "teach the sons of Israel all the statutes which the LORD has spoken to them by the hand of Moses." Thus, God's promise attached to the Fifth Commandment actually applies to all of the Ten Commandments and to the whole of God's Word.

Many of God's promises pertain to this world and apply to all of God's Word. What are some examples of these promises?

> *If you will carefully listen to the voice of the LORD your God, and will do that which is right in His sight, and will give ear to His commandments, and keep all His laws, I will put none of these diseases upon you, which I have brought upon the Egyptians; for I am the LORD who heals you."* —*Exodus 15:26*

> *You shall not bow down to their gods, nor serve them. And you shall not do according to their works. But you shall surely pull them down, and surely you shall smash their images. And you shall serve the LORD your God, and He shall bless your bread and your water. And I will take sickness away from the midst of you. Nothing shall cast their young, nor be barren in your land. The number of your days I will fulfill."* —*Exodus 23:24-26*

These are just a few of many examples of God's promises to Israel. The point is that obedience to God's Word results in health and longevity for God's people.

To implement this agenda the Lord charged parents to teach their children the Word of God. Families are to educate their children, to teach them biblical values and skills necessary for life. In biblical times businesses were family owned, so education included preparation to work in a family business.

WEALTH

Health and longevity were not all that God promised either. Obedience to God's promises also provide an increase of material wealth for His people. I'm not talking about the contemporary version of the wealth and prosperity gospel. Your personal material wealth will not increase by simply directing your tithe to *me* or to any anyone else. In fact, that whole approach to the Bible is faulty because it issues from greed. The greed of those who teach the contemporary prosperity gospel infects others who then tithe in order to get rich themselves. That's not what Scripture teaches.

Nowhere does Scripture promise to make anyone in particular rich. However, Scripture does promise to increase the wealth and security of faithful families and societies. How? Through inheritance, by keeping honestly earned wealth and property in the family and by increasing the number of wealthy families in a society. Obedience to Scripture will raise the "water level" (so to speak) of the economy, which will in turn raise the "boats" (economic level) of most people, some more than others, of course.

In the Bible the family is the primary economic unit, and some extended families grew quite large. The Bible does not encourage personal wealth apart from family responsibility. The Bible teaches that families are to be cooperative by living in submission to God's authority, which is exercised through the head of the household. It is not that the head of the household gets to do whatever *he* wants, but that the head of the household has an increased responsibly to be obedient to Scripture because he has responsibility for his family as well as for himself.

Part of that responsibility is to care for and educate his children. Part of that responsibility was also to care for and honor his aging parents. The strength of the biblical family is that it provides for its members whenever they need it, as young children and as aging grandparents. By caring for young and old, families provided necessary social services that benefit the greater society in many ways. And because the cost of these social services are handled within the family (or extended family), the cost is considerably less than having them done by private or state service organizations (businesses).

Because the family was the primary economic unit in Bible times, all business was family oriented business. Families had primary responsibility for and control over their businesses and property. That does not mean that every family member had equal say in the family business. Rather, authority was tied to ability and experience. Generally speaking, it means that business practices and procedures were determined by families, not by civil courts.

However, when business or property disputes arose between families those disputes were adjudicated by the elders at the city gates. For instance, property was bought and sold at the city gate, where the elders could serve as witnesses. Here we find the roots of civil law and order.

QUESTIONS

This raises many questions. Wouldn't such a family-based economic system lend itself to the perversion of justice by elevating the family unit as the most powerful element in society? With business comes wealth, and with wealth comes power. It seems that over time the power of the family unit would produce Mafia-like family related organizations that would exploit every advantage to increase their own power and wealth. All of their energy would be put in service to maintain the family business and relationships. It would be quite easy and natural for such families to pit themselves against other families and even against civil law in order to maximize their own power and wealth. Indeed, much of history is filled with these kinds of struggles.

However, Scripture anticipated this situation and provided clear direction to deal with it. God's Word requires that family commitment to God's law be above its commitment to its own members. Biblical law is above family ties.

THE REBELLIOUS SON

Consider the case of the rebellious son.

> If a man has a son who is stubborn and rebels, who will not obey his fathers voice or his mothers voice, even when they have chastened him he will not listen to them, then his father and his mother shall lay hold on him and bring him out to the elders of his city, and to the gate of his place. And they shall say to the elders of his city, this son of ours is stubborn and rebellious. He will not obey our voice. He is a glutton and a drunkard. And all the men of his city shall stone him with stones so that he dies. So shall you put evil away from you, and all Israel shall hear and fear."   —Deuteronomy 21:18-21

First of all, we need to get beyond our modern offense with this story, so that we can learn the lesson it teaches. Too often, people reject what seems to them to be an injustice, and dismiss any genuine consideration of this story. We must remember that we are not in the position to judge God's Word. God is just, regardless of what we may think. Therefore, it behooves us to put aside our petty concerns and learn what the Lord is teaching through this story. What lessons or principles can we find here?

The rebellious son received the same penalty as the blasphemer because rebellion against parental authority is equivalent to rebellion against God, against God's authority, and against God's social order. Rebellion against authority will eventually result in the destruction of social order itself and bring large-scale suffering and death to society.

Thus, biblical law places less value on the person who rebels against God's social order, and more value upon God's social order itself because the destruction of social order will eventually result in the death of the society.[3]

This case serves to demonstrate that blood kinship was to be in submission to biblical law, that biblical law has precedence over family relationships. The family was the foundation of society and the basic economic unit, but it was not above the law. God's law, not blood ties, must govern. Family relationships were/are not above the law. God is not a respecter of persons. "To have respect of persons in judgment is not good" (Proverbs 24:23). "God is no respecter of persons" (Acts 10:34). "There is no respect of persons with God" (Romans 2:11).

APPLICATION

The truth is that this kind of situation will never come up where the Fifth Commandment is implemented. The lesson here is not that God is cruel, or that disobedient children should be stoned to death—although punishment for sin is necessary because God is just. If punishment does not follow sin, then God cannot possibly be just. Rather, the real lesson here is that the Lord has graciously and mercifully provided a law that will generally prevent this unfortunate situation from happening at all, and will preserve His social order.

God manifested His grace and mercy even more by receiving Christ's atonement on the cross for all of the sins His people would ever commit, save one.

Here is how it works in the light of Christ. If one of God's children failed to obey the Fifth Commandment and grew to be a glutton and a drunkard, in spite of his parents' discipline, God's forgiving grace would apply to that individual's sin as he confessed Christ or received Christ in true repentance. In other words, Christ's death on the cross paid for the sins of His people. Thus, the punishment for such a disobedient child would be unnecessary unless the child spurns the forgiveness that Christ provided. If the child turns his back on God's forgiveness provided by Christ on the cross, then he invites God's wrath and the punishment for his sin upon himself. But the first order of things applies to the grace and mercy of God's forgiveness. The very first thing that God does in Christ is to offer forgiveness for repentance.

The usefulness of a law like this is not found in its execution, which would always be a tragedy of extreme error. Rather, the usefulness would be the deterrence that it could provide to rebellious chil-

---

3   I am not suggesting that rebellious children be condemned to death and any suggestion of such is patently untrue. I'm simply trying to discern the lesson in this case study.

dren to take their parents more seriously. One of the difficulties of parental discipline is that it is difficult to engage because parents love their children, and tend to err on the side of excessive tolerance, mercy and forgiveness. So it could serve to "back up" the authority of parents by providing a potential consequence which parents are not able to ameliorate or control. In my opinion, the ideal situation would be to have such a law on the books, but not be enforceable. Making sense of a law like this is only understandable in the light of Christ, from a regenerate perspective that is able to see the comprehensiveness of God's plan.

The point is that God's amazing grace is at work in the lives of people—in spite of their disobedience. Christ has interposed Himself between God and sinners. Christ received the punishment for the sins of His people. God's law is honored because punishment for sin has been fully exercised upon Christ on the cross. God's people do not receive punishment for their sin—Christ has already received it! Rather, God's children receive God's mercy and forgiveness as they turn to Christ in repentance. This is the proper use of such a law, to reveal the grace and mercy of Christ for rebellious sinners.

To turn our backs on Christ is, then, to walk willingly into the gaping jaws of hell and eternal damnation. To turn our backs on Christ serves to glorify God's justice. God's integrity is then revealed by the exercise of His vengeance against sin.

Thus, God's order, God's authority, God's plan of salvation fully engages His law, both its punishments and its rewards. It has been said that God has a plan for your life, and indeed He does. God's salvation plan is that His people will live in submission to His Word and receive His blessings. Christ already received the punishment for all the sins of all of God's people.

On the other hand, those who reject God's Word and refuse to submit to His law will receive the just punishment for their own sins because they refuse to accept Christ's payment for it in their stead. Thus, no one is excluded from God's salvation plan. God has a plan for believers and unbelievers alike.

Have you turned to Christ? Are you resting in Christ, resting in God's Sabbath in Christ, resting in the assurance of salvation by the blood of Christ? If not, I pray that God will change your mind, open your heart, and give you the wisdom of submission to His Word.

The issue of the rebellious son in this biblical story is not really about this particular person, but it is about *you* and *me*, about rebellious sinners one and all. The consequences of rebellion will be paid sooner or later. They cannot be avoided. There is only one solution to the problem, and that is Christ.

Vengeance

You shall not kill.   —*Exodus 20:13*

The Sixth Commandment has been instituted in order to curtail the human instinct to take revenge. Deuteronomy 32:35 tells us in no uncertain terms that "Vengeance and retribution belong to (the Lord). Their foot shall slide in time, for the day of their calamity is at hand, and the things that shall come on them make haste." That fact is reiterated in Psalm 94:1, "O LORD God, to whom vengeance belongeth; O God, to whom vengeance belongeth, shew thyself" (KJV).

God's authority and responsibility to exercise vengeance Himself is also spoken of in Isaiah 35:4, "Say to those of a hasty heart, Be strong, fear not; behold, your God will come with vengeance, with the full dealing of God. He will come and save you." In addition to claiming vengeance for Himself, we see that God's vengeance is part and parcel of God's salvation. Scripture places vengeance and salvation together as twin aspects of God's judgment.

> *The Spirit of the Lord Jehovah is on Me; because the Lord has anointed Me to preach the Gospel to the poor; He has sent Me to bind up the broken-hearted, to proclaim liberty to the captives, and the opening of the prison to those who are bound; to preach the acceptable year of the Lord and the day of vengeance of our God; to comfort all who mourn; to appoint to those who mourn in Zion, to give to them beauty for ashes, the oil of joy for mourning, the mantle of praise for the spirit of heaviness; so that they might be called trees of righteousness, the planting of the Lord, that He might be glorified.*   —*Isaiah 61: 1-3*

ONE COIN, TWO SIDES

Vengeance is the other side of salvation. Thus, God's vengeance cannot be separated from salvation because both vengeance and salvation are products of God's character. Perfect justice brings results in vengeance (or retribution) and perfect mercy results in salvation.

By issuing the Sixth Commandment God forbids people from taking vengeance into their own hands. In essence, it forbids people from taking the law into their own hands, for that is what taking vengeance always comes to. "Repay no one evil for evil. Provide things honest in the sight of all men. If it is possible, as far as is in you, seeking peace with all men. not avenging yourselves, beloved, but giving place to wrath; for it is written, 'Vengeance is Mine, I will repay, says the Lord'" (Romans 12:17-19).

The primary purpose of the Sixth Commandment is to forbid the murdering of another person. It does not forbid the slaughtering of animals for food or hunting, or the taking of life by the state as punishment for crime. This commandment does not justify vegetarianism or pacifism. Nor does it apply to self-defense or defending others who are under attack. It is simply a command against taking personal revenge. The Lord knows that the purpose and ultimate outcome of revenge is death, inflicted by taking the law into one's own hands. Those who seek revenge serve lawlessness and death.

In addition, the implications of this command are not limited to the taking of life, but naturally extend to all activities that promote or contribute toward death. In other words, the commandment also forbids beating someone to an inch of his life, but not actually killing him. Why? Because any revenge that is taken serves the purposes of death and lawlessness. The hate that animates human vengeance loves and serves death and destruction. Proverbs 8:36 tells us that "he who sins against (the Lord) wrongs his own soul; all who hate (God) love death."

PROMOTE LIFE

The positive statement of the Sixth Commandment insists that all our personal activities and actions should serve and promote life, social order, and God's law. The command has a wide range of positive applications regarding health, wealth, and longevity. God's sanction of life guides Christian attitudes regarding the totality of human life, including the weaknesses and dependencies of both embryonic and senile existence. The positive injunctions of the Sixth Commandment concern life as a whole, not the mere pragmatics of personal or social usefulness. The prohibitions against murder and revenge bring into focus the positive concern to nurture and sustain all human life.

After a generation of environmental indoctrination, people today ask if human life is to be valued above animal and vegetable life. They ask the question because they believe that the world is overcrowded, that there is a scarcity of available resources, and that man is a mere animal. For a generation or more, public education has taught that humanity is just another species, that man is not substantially different than any other species on the earth.

However, such beliefs are not grounded in Scripture, and are therefore false. Thus, the question itself is false, and at best poorly stated. Those who have been indoctrinated into a belief in evolution and the values that evolution teaches cannot even conceive of the appropriate questions to ask, much less the answers. Understanding God's answers requires a functional biblical vocabulary, familiarity with biblical categories of thought and a regenerate perspective. This is why the ungodly find biblical answers so unsatisfying.

Nonetheless, Scripture teaches that God indeed values man above all other creatures. God created man in His own image and made Him steward of the earth. Man's position as steward is not of his own making. Rather, it is a position assigned to him by the Lord Himself, and therefore, carries both the authority of the Lord and includes all of the various responsibilities that are given by the Lord.

But while there is a special value attached to humanity by the Lord, it is utter foolishness to fail to understand that Scripture also teaches that human life depends upon animal and vegetable life. Humanity is not independent from the created order, but dependent upon it. Life is indeed an interrelated whole. However, the whole is not randomly ordered. Everything indicates that there is a specific order of being or relationships between and among microorganisms, plants, animals, and even the macro systems like weather. Scripture tells us that God created and directs that order. Thus, to violate that order is to court death.

SYMBIOTIC

One of the wonders of this world is the fact of the interconnections and interrelationships between the many expressions of life, what the Bible calls "kinds." For instance, bees and flowers require each other. The bees pollinate the flowers and the flowers produce food for the bee—and for us. Thus, responsible stewardship of the earth means maintaining and caring for these many natural interrelationships. The stewardship of the earth requires the full consideration of the so-called balance of nature. That balance requires responsible, Godly stewardship by man, according to the Word of God. The purpose of the earth itself centers upon man's life in the Lord. All of creation exists to glorify God.

However, sin and the Fall have marred the expression of God's glory, particularly in man. Thus, Christ has brought redemption to His people in order to restore the right expression of God's glory in the lives of His people, and through them, to all of creation.

New Testament Support

The order of creation and the admonition against revenge was renewed and refined by Jesus in the Sermon on the Mount.

> *You have heard that it was said to the ancients, 'You shall not kill'—*
> *and, 'Whoever shall kill shall be liable to the judgment.' But I say to*
> *you that whoever is angry with his brother without a cause shall be*
> *liable to the judgment. And whoever shall say to his brother, Raca,*
> *shall be liable to the sanhedrin; but whoever shall say, Fool! shall be*
> *liable to be thrown into the fire of hell.* —Matthew 5:21-22

Jesus makes our responsibility even clearer by revealing that the sources of revenge are hate and anger. Thus, obedience to the Sixth Commandment requires that we put an end to hate and anger. Jesus recovered the real meaning of faithfulness by restating God's demand for faithfulness from the control of our outward personal behavior to the control of our inward personal attitude, from the level of actions to the level of thoughts, and from thoughts to desires. Jesus said that not only is wrong action sinful, but wrong thought is also sinful.

Thought and action tend to follow desire. Desire leads thought and action. People are attracted to whatever they desire. Desire leads, thought mitigates, and action embraces. Thus, true faithfulness is not simply doing what is right, doing good works or deeds. Nor is faithfulness merely right thinking, not simply reading Scripture or contemplating the things of the Lord. While right thoughts and actions are engaged by faithful Christians, the essence of real faithfulness is genuinely *desiring* God, wanting for yourself what the Lord wants for you. Actions can be faked, thoughts can be wrong or insincere. But the genuine desire to actually please God is the heart of faithfulness.

Pleasing God means, among other things, not taking vengeance into your own hands. It means living life according to God's Word, and taking responsibility for yourself and your role in the stewardship of God's earth. To please God we must apply the Sixth Commandment and its positive implications to all of life. This commandment requires more than the mere avoidance of murder.

ADULTERY

You shall not commit adultery. —*Exodus 20:14*

The Lᴏʀᴅ also said to me in the days of Josiah the king, Have you seen that which backsliding Israel has done? She has gone up on every high mountain and under every green tree, and has fornicated there. And I said after she had done all these things, Turn to Me! But she did not return. And her treacherous sister Judah saw it. And I saw, when for all the causes for which backsliding Israel committed adultery, I sent her away and gave a bill of divorce to her, yet her treacherous sister Judah did not fear, but she went and whored, she also. And it happened, from the folly of her whoredom, she defiled the land and fornicated with stones and stocks. And yet for all this her treacherous sister Judah has not turned to Me with her whole heart, but with falsehood, says the Lᴏʀᴅ. And the Lᴏʀᴅ said to me, The backsliding Israel has justified herself more than treacherous Judah. Go and cry these words toward the north, and say, Return, O backsliding Israel, says the Lᴏʀᴅ; and I will not cause My anger to fall on you; for I am merciful, says the Lᴏʀᴅ, and I will not keep anger forever. Only acknowledge your iniquity, that you have sinned against the Lᴏʀᴅ your God and have scattered your ways to the strangers under every green tree, and you have not obeyed My voice, says the Lᴏʀᴅ. Turn, O backsliding sons, says the Lᴏʀᴅ; for I am married to you; and I will take you one from a city, and two from a family, and I will bring you to Zion. And I will give you shepherds according to My heart, who shall feed you with knowledge and understanding. And it will be when you have multiplied and increased in the land, in those days, says the Lᴏʀᴅ, they shall say no more, The ark of the covenant of the Lᴏʀᴅ! Nor shall it come to mind; nor shall they remember it; nor shall they visit it; nor shall it be made any more. At that time they shall

call Jerusalem the throne of the Lord; and all nations shall be
gathered to it, to the name of the Lord, to Jerusalem. Nor shall they
walk any more after the stubbornness of their evil heart. In those
days the house of Judah shall walk with the house of Israel, and they
shall come together out of the land of the north to the land that I
have given for an inheritance to your fathers.   *—Jeremiah 3:6-18*

U nderstanding this commandment is not difficult. Yet, it remains one of the most vilified and violated commandments in history. The commandment intends to limit sexual interaction to husband and wife. Period. All other sexual engagement is forbidden. Everyone knows whether or not s/he is married, and to whom s/he is married. That should be the end of the matter. But it is not.

COLLEGE

The power of sin to rationalize our own beliefs and behaviors is astounding. We live in a day of complete defiance of this particular commandment. In fact, people today pride themselves upon their violation of this commandment and call it enlightenment or freedom from the repressive norms of the past. Many—if not most—contemporary institutions actually promote, and often even formally teach, the violation of the Seventh Commandment. The most damnable are institutions of so-called higher learning—colleges and universities. On today's campuses the witch's brew of freedom from parental oversight, raging hormones, easy access to drugs and alcohol, and outright encouragement by the social mores of professors and administrators, provides a toxic incentive to engage illicit sexual activity that is difficult to resist.

More often than not, young adults are thrown into an environment of sexual experimentation and alcoholic indulgence in the name of education. Parents blindly support such activity because they refuse to believe that the world they live in could be so depraved. Thus, the forces of destruction and damnation thrive as they feed off of the love and charity of well-meaning but blind-sided parents, who in many cases continue to claim their own Christianity while at the same time deny the grip that Satan has upon them and upon—if not through— their children.

Nonetheless, the biblical commandment itself is clear and not subject to misunderstanding. It is simply set aside in favor of personal preferences. The reestablishment of this commandment in our day and age is, therefore, not simply a matter of education. Biblical morality cannot be taught, as if it were a science. We should realize by now that education itself does not produce godly people, nor even moral people.

Education only makes people smarter. Smarter sinners then find more creative and intelligent ways to sin.

God's Concern

Nonetheless, it may be helpful to understand why God is so concerned about adultery. Adultery differs from fornication in that adultery is a violation of the marriage covenant, where fornication—sex between unmarried people, which is also forbidden—is not the same kind of covenantal violation.

God's statute against adultery serves to protect our human understanding and commitment to covenantal commitments. God is concerned because our relationship with Him is a covenantal relationship. His concern is that disregard for any covenantal relationship promotes a similar disregard for all covenantal relationships. Similarly, as circular as it may sound, the practice of sin encourages the practice of sin. The more a person sins, the easier sin becomes.

The reason that God deals so harshly with adultery is that by the time people find themselves entangled in it, they have long since abandoned their covenant with God. In order to get into a position to have an adulterous relationship requires lying and cheating. Adultery violates the marriage covenant. Lies are made to create a time and place. Both parties then dishonor their marriage covenant, their promises of faithfulness. Seldom is adultery practiced with the knowledge and consent of the uninvolved marriage partner. However, on the occasions that it is, it is no less a function of deceit and dishonor because it still violates the exclusivity of marriage itself.

Adultery

Adultery also requires taking the Lord's name in vain. To disobey a particular law is to ignore and undermine the authority of law in general. Thus, adultery defames God's character as Law-giver. To violate the marriage covenant requires the breaking of God's law. Further, by breaking the law people deny the authority of the law, and the right of the law maker to make law. Thus, God's character as Law-giver is defamed.

We are not simply talking about the Ten Commandments here. Adultery—and indeed all sin—also requires the violation of the most important commandment, as Jesus Himself testified, "you shall love the Lord your God with all your heart, and with all your soul, and with all your mind, and with all your strength" (Mark 12:30). To love the Lord means to honor and obey Him. Thus, by the time that an adulterous relationship is consummated, the parties involved have utterly trashed their covenantal relationship with God.

To put it positively, the best protection against sin is to honor and maintain a covenantal relationship with the Lord. Putting the Lord and His Word aside, with regard to any matter, is itself the first act of sin. The effort to set the Lord aside, to ignore God, fuels the progression of sin in our lives and in our world. The Seventh Commandment is not merely concerned with sexual relationships, but primarily with our relationship with the Lord Himself. Thus, Scripture speaks of adultery in the broadest sense. Those who abandon or forget the Lord are spoken of as adulterers. Adultery is first and foremost a denial of God's covenant.

Jesus said, "An evil and adulterous generation seeks after a sign. And there shall be no sign given to it except the sign of the prophet Jonah" (Matthew 12:39). An "adulterous generation" here refers not merely to the fact of illicit sexual relationships, but of the abandonment of God's covenant. When the covenant with God is broken, it is broken by man. God will not break His covenant with humanity. He has promised to sustain His covenant eternally. God does not lie, and will not negate His Word. His covenant with humanity will never expire.

That covenant, of course, involves more than the salvation of the God's people. It also involves the damnation of unrepentant sinners. This fullness of God's covenant is taught throughout Scripture. People don't usually have any problem with the salvation side of God's covenant, but often struggle with the damnation side. Nonetheless, it is everywhere in Scripture.

The Lord Himself speaks through Malachi 3:5, "I will come near you to judgment. And I will be a swift witness against the sorcerers, and against the adulterers, and against false swearers, and against those who extort from the hired laborer's wages, and turning away the widow, and the orphan, the alien, and not fearing Me, says the Lord of hosts." People are aware that the God of the Old Testament often spoke of such things. But God's promise of salvation and damnation, is not just an Old Testament teaching. Similarly, Paul testifies in Ephesians 5:5-7, "For you know this, that no fornicator, or unclean person, or covetous one (who is an idolater), has any inheritance in the kingdom of Christ and of God. Let no man deceive you with vain words, for because of these things the wrath of God comes upon the children of disobedience. Therefore do not be partakers with them." Those without any inheritance in God's kingdom are bound for hell. God is no less the God of vengeance in the New Testament than He was in the Old.

DAMNED BY JESUS

Jesus Himself confirmed the doctrine of damnation. "The Son of man shall send out His angels, and they shall gather out of His kingdom all things that offend, and those who do iniquity, and shall cast them into a furnace of fire. There shall be wailing and gnashing of teeth" (Matthew 13:41-42). Thus, whatever response people make to the Lord will be dealt with according to the dictates of God's covenant promises—salvation for all who turn to the Lord, and damnation for all who turn away from Him. The Bible speaks of no middle ground, no neutral position, no other choice. The issue is not whether or not we like this teaching. The issue is whether or not Scripture teaches it, and clearly it does.

The practical application of God's commandment against adultery is easy to understand. There can be no doubt about whether or not a particular person has violated it or not, at least not in his or her own mind. However, the world in which we live will do all it can to nullify and discount the value of God's Word. Every effort is made to convince people that God and His Word—the Bible—are mere fables, or outdated, or otherwise not in effect in the world in which we currently live. Our fallen nature makes it easy for people to believe such lies. People want to believe it.

Today, all sexual activity is portrayed as easy, safe, harmless, and normal. While those who so portray it concern themselves primarily with the physical or mechanical aspects of sex, they deny much medical evidence to the contrary. It is even suggested that people are more emotionally healthy when sex is freely engaged without the unnecessary baggage of moral restriction. The desire of sinners to justify themselves has led to a self-centered psychology that has completely redefined human morality in terms of its own selfish desires. No concern is given to God or to the eternal truth of God's Word.

Application of the Seventh Commandment is not a matter of understanding, but of obedience. People may fool themselves and their friends, but they cannot fool God. He knows what people actually believe and think, and His justice will prevail.

THEFT

You shall not steal.   —*Exodus 20:15*

And when He had come into Jerusalem, all the city was moved,
saying, Who is this? And the crowd said, This is Jesus the prophet,
from Nazareth of Galilee. And Jesus went into the temple of God and
cast out all those who sold and bought in the temple, and overthrew
the tables of the money-changers, and the seats of those who sold
doves. And He said to them, It is written, "My house shall be called
the house of prayer"; but you have made it a den of thieves.
            —*Matthew 21:10-13*

As the Seventh Commandment concerns marriage, the Eighth
Commandment concerns dominion, or responsible stewardship
of the earth and all of its gifts. Theft indicates a false understanding about the nature of reality, a false idea about property and
ownership. The truth is that everything belongs to God and we are His
stewards. We can be good stewards or bad stewards, honest stewards
or dishonest stewards, but stewards we are.

There are many kinds of theft, and all are covered in this
commandment. Building on Deuteronomy 22, Calvin said,

> *If an agent or an indolent steward wastes the substance of his*
> *employer, or does not give due heed to the management of his*
> *property; if he unjustly squanders or luxuriously wastes the means*
> *entrusted to him; if a servant holds his master in derision, divulges*
> *his secrets, or in any way is treacherous to his life or his goods; if, on*
> *the other hand, a master cruelly torments his household, he is guilty*
> *of theft before God; since every one who, in the exercise of his*
> *calling, performs not what he owes to others, keeps back, or makes*
> *away with what does not belong to him" (Calvin's Institutes 2:8).*

The Westminster Catechism says that the Eighth Commandment requires the "lawful procuring and furthering of the wealth and the outward estate of others and ourselves." Paul counseled Timothy, "if anyone does not provide for his own, and especially his family, he has denied the faith and is worse than an infidel" (1 Timothy 5:8). The Catechism adds further clarification by saying that this commandment forbids whatever unjustly hinders our own or our neighbor's wealth or outward estate.

Paul, speaking of the power of repentance, said:

> *For you ought to put off the old man (according to your way of living before) who is corrupt according to the deceitful lusts, and be renewed in the spirit of your mind. And you should put on the new man, who according to God was created in righteousness and true holiness. Therefore putting away lying, let each man speak truth with his neighbor, for we are members of one another. Be angry, and do not sin. Do not let the sun go down upon your wrath, neither give place to the Devil. Let him who stole steal no more, but rather let him labor, working with his hands the thing which is good, so that he may have something to give to him who needs. Let not any filthy word go out of your mouth, but if any is good to building up in respect of need, that it may give grace to the ones hearing. And do not grieve the Holy Spirit of God, by whom you are sealed until the day of redemption"* —Ephesians 4:22-30

NEEDS VERSUS WANTS

The act of theft or of irresponsible stewardship gives priority to one's own thoughts rather than to God's Word. To be a steward means being responsible for someone else's property. To be God's stewards means to care for God's property as God has instructed. Not even genuine personal need can take priority over God's law because the owner of the property determines how the steward is to care for it.

We easily confuse our own needs with our wants, and end up in covetousness. It is easy to believe that we need or deserve something. But doing so requires that we place ourselves above God and His Word and act as self-determined arbiters of the world's goods. The Lord expects His people to respect the life, marriage, property, and reputation of our neighbors because He has commanded it. No other reason is necessary. And furthermore, God's law always takes priority over human conditions, including what we might think are our own needs. God's Word takes precedence over human need.

RESTITUTION

Scripture speaks much about making restitution for wrongs committed, and restitution comes to play a special role in the Eighth Commandment. However, the effort to correct wrongs that have been done is not limited to theft, but runs throughout Scripture. We are to do everything we can to fix what we have done wrong.

However, human restoration is impossible when God Himself has been wronged. When wrongs are committed against God, our only restitution is Jesus Christ, who alone can restore sinful people to a holy God. How can we make restitution for having other gods? We cannot. How can we make restitution for making graven images? How can we make up for broken Sabbaths?

Sins against God can only be made right through Jesus Christ. We can renounce false gods. We can smash graven images. We can promise to honor the Sabbath. But the damage has been done, and cannot be undone apart from the propitiation of sin itself by Jesus Christ on the cross. It can only be propitiated by Jesus Christ because we do not have the inclination or the ability to do so apart from Him.

When our sin involves other people we can begin to address it. But even then, restoration apart from Christ is impossible. How can we restore a life that has been taken? We cannot. The Bible commands a life for a life, blood for blood—and such actions help institute social justice. Nonetheless, the life of the victim is still gone. How can we restore lost virginity? We cannot. People talk about secondary virginity after conversion, and that is good. But secondary virginity is not really virginity at all. It is really only playing with words, but it makes the best of a bad situation and so it is useful.

However, when we come to the Eight Commandment things are different. Stolen property can be restored. Here restitution between people becomes more doable. Even the unsaved can restore stolen or damaged property, or pay for it. They probably will not do so unless civil government forces them. But here restitution in fact becomes possible and more practical.

Every sin is a demonstration of human sinfulness. And every attempt to restore ourselves or to make up for what we have done apart from Christ is nothing more than self-righteousness. Sinners cannot make amends to a holy God. Apart from Christ this world of sinners is completely lost and helpless.

UNIVERSAL APPLICATION

We must remember and realize that God's promises have been given to humanity as a whole. God's promises, God's laws apply to *every* human being, not just to the saved, but to everyone. And here we see an example of this fact in that God demands restoration of stolen property. Actually, all of God's commandments apply to everyone, the faithful and the faithless, but it is easier to see the truth of this fact here in the Eighth Commandment. The law against theft is universal.

Of course, the application of the Eighth Commandment involves much more than the restoration of stolen property. The application begins with what we might call preventative maintenance. To waste or squander one's own resources is to waste or squander God's property because everything ultimately belongs to God. Thus, poor management is a kind of theft. It steals resources away from family, employer, customers, neighbors, and from the society as a whole. Thus, the responsibilities of the Eighth Commandment include learning and practicing good household and business management.

There are two aspects of this kind of management. One involves saving, the other involves spending. Good management requires that resources be conserved by not carelessly spending everything you have. This requires that resources be conserved through price comparison and purchasing quality merchandise. The practice of unnecessary or luxury spending must also be carefully monitored. It is not that such spending is biblically immoral, but that it should only be engaged when people are able to do so without going into debt. Making or purchasing shoddy or inferior merchandise is also a violation of this commandment because inferior merchandise squanders God's resources.

Debt

Debt spending by individuals, businesses, or governments is the most common abuse of the Eighth Commandment. Scripture does not forbid debt because it is sometimes necessary. However, Scripture regularly and strongly counsels against being in debt. If God's people are to be free, they must first be debt free. Debt has always been a means of slavery. "The rich rules over the poor, and the borrower is servant to the lender" (Proverbs 22:7). The primary definition of *ebed*, the Hebrew word translated here as *servant*, is **slave**. Indeed, a person in debt is a person in slavery to the holder of his note. Again, there are times when debt is necessary, but it should never be a regular practice. Here we find that contemporary household and business practices are at variance with Scripture in this regard. Who should we believe? Our banker, or the God of Scripture?

Salary

James 5:4 counsels against another kind of theft, "Behold, the hire of the laborers reaping your fields cry out, being kept back by you. And the cries of those who have reaped have entered into the ears of the Lord of hosts." To fail to pay honest wages, fair wages, decent wages to workers is another violation of this commandment. It is a form of theft.

What can you do to practice the Eighth Commandment? Do everything you can to stay out of debt by good management of your assets. That means working hard to earn and conserve resources in whatever field the Lord has placed you—school, home, or work. Make good use of your time by dedicating yourself fully to the Lord. "See then that you walk circumspectly, not as fools, but as wise, redeeming the time, because the days are evil. Therefore do not be unwise, but understand what the will of the Lord is" (Ephesians 5:15-17).

Time

Time is the most precious resource we have. Wasting time is another violation of this commandment. That does not mean that we should spend all of our time working. But it does mean that we should use all of our time in the service of God's purposes. Sabbath observance, a regular cycle of work and rest, is the best way to make sure that our time conforms to God's purposes.

Thus when the Lord forbids stealing, He commands proper use of the many gifts He has bestowed upon us. The commandment against theft is actually a commandment to engage in responsible stewardship. Blessed be the Lord.

TRUTH

You shall not bear false witness against your neighbor.

—Exodus 20:16

To understand what this Commandment means we must first discuss what it does not mean in order to flush from our minds some misunderstandings and false presumptions that confuse and lead people astray.

Too many people interpret this commandment to mean that they should always tell the truth in every situation. But that is not what it says. Don't get me wrong, telling the truth is almost always a good thing. But apart from God's Word, even telling the truth can lead people astray. Even the truth can be used for wicked purposes. Satan not only perverts the truth, but he uses truth for evil purposes. When Satan tempted Jesus in the wilderness he said, "If you are the Son of God, cast yourself down. For it is written, 'He shall give His angels charge concerning You, and in their hands they shall bear You up, lest at any time You dash Your foot against a stone'" (Matthew 4:6). Satan knows the truth, and quotes Scripture, but his purposes are evil.

Contrasting those who follow God and those who don't, Proverbs 11:12-13 says, "One despising his friend lacks heart, but a man of understanding remains silent. One going with slander is a revealer of secrets, but the faithful of spirit keeps the matter hidden." To speak rashly, even if truthfully, can destroy friendships. Whereas those who slander and gossip often use the truth out of context or with malice, deception can be used for good purposes. God Himself allows for deception in the accomplishment of His purposes.

Scripture tells us that faithfulness sometimes requires keeping a matter hidden. God Himself does not reveal all things alike to all people. Jesus Himself prayed, "I thank You, O Father, Lord of Heaven and earth, because You have hidden these things from the sophisticated and cunning, and revealed them to babes. Even so, Father, for so it seemed good in Your sight" (Matthew 11:25-26). God doesn't conceal everything. For instance, God does not conceal what is necessary for the salvation of His people, yet in His wisdom He sometimes hides and conceals the truth from those who would misuse and abuse it.

The Ninth Commandment is not about always telling the truth in every situation, as it is often misunderstood to be. Rather, it is about not using falsehood against your neighbors. It is about using the truth in the service of God. There is an important difference. Look at it again, "You shall not bear false witness against your neighbor."

It says nothing about always telling the truth. The idea that it means always telling the truth is an inference, a deduction, or conclusion that people draw from it. But it is a false conclusion. Drawing such a conclusion provides a perfect case of people hearing the Word of God, and then applying an untrue meaning or interpretation to it, making it say what they want it to say, what they think it ought to say. When this happens human meaning is substituted for God's meaning, our own thoughts are substituted for God's thoughts.

RAHAB THE LYING WHORE

Rahab provides a case in point. Rahab is one of the great saints of the faith. Scripture testifies that "by faith the harlot Rahab did not perish with those who did not believe, when she had received the spies with peace" (Hebrews 11:31). When Rahab lied to the king's soldiers about the Israelite spies she did not violate this commandment. Rather, Scripture repeatedly honors her because of her courage and good judgment. Her deception in the face of danger was an act of vital faithfulness, not an affront to God's commands. The point is not that God saved Rahab in spite of her lies, but that she is honored for faithfully concealing the truth in the service of the Lord. Understanding the Ninth Commandment requires an understanding of Rahab's faithfulness.

People fail to fully appreciate this commandment because they want to make life simpler than it really is. People want life to be easy and inexpensive. Such people have little concern for doing what is right, they just want to get by without any difficulties, even when the difficulties themselves are gifts of grace for sanctification. God gives people situations and circumstances for their own good that are often perceived to be difficulties. They are given to help people grow and mature. Difficulties make people strong. They keep people sharp and alert. When life is easy, people grow fat and lazy. But because people like to be lazy, they often don't fully appreciate what God gives them. People don't like it when God gives them difficulties, even when those difficulties prove to be good for them in the long run.

GOD'S SOVEREIGNTY

If God is truly sovereign, and He is, then all things come from the hand of God. This teaching, the doctrine of God's sovereignty, disturbs many people because they cannot accept the reality that their personal failure to appreciate something does not make it bad or evil. God is not the author of evil, yet evil things do happen, so how are we to understand it when they do?

We must realize that God makes good use of the evil that is produced by Satan and by sinners. Even the evil in the world, which God Himself is not responsible for, serves His purposes. For instance, when Joseph revealed himself to his brothers as they sought refuge from the famine, remembering how they sold him into slavery, he said, "But as for you, you thought evil against me, but God meant it for good, to bring to pass, as it is this day, to save a great many people alive" (Genesis 50:20).

One of the good things that comes from evil is the destruction of evil and the punishment of sinners. "The wicked is snared by the transgression of his lips, but the just shall come out of trouble" (Proverbs 12:13). Wickedness itself often supplies its own punishment. If God failed to punish sinners, He would be both unjust and not perfectly good, and thus not God.

The difficulty comes about because we resist thinking of ourselves and our friends as sinners. Or because we value our own understanding of the nature of good above God's Word. People stand in judgment of God when they reject Him or reject the gifts He gives. To disagree with God is to value yourself above God.

People would rather slander God than face the truth, so they turn God's Word into humanistic moral platitudes that can be both appreciated for their beauty and at the same time ignored because of their uselessness. Understanding the Ninth Commandment to mean that people should never lie provides a stunning example of this tendency. It sounds so noble to strive to always tell the truth, but it is both foolish nonsense and impossible. Such an understanding becomes an easily ignorable platitude because it cannot be done. To always tell the truth requires knowing the truth perfectly, and no one does. Nonetheless, people pride themselves on their noble effort to strive to always tell the truth, while at the same time they discount their lies because of the impossibility to always tell the truth. Thus, the result of this kind of platitudinization of Scripture is pride and self-justification.

Scripture honors Rahab because of her commitment to the Lord, and to His people. Her deceit protected what God valued. It protected God's people and furthered God plans. There is no higher good than to value what God values and serve His purposes.

People complain that Rahab sided with the Jews against her own city, and therefore her action was evil. Or they complain against God's authority and command to destroy Jericho. They accuse God of immorality!

However, real immorality is disagreeing with God. Biblical morality is not doing what *we* think is right, but is obedience to God, to Scripture. In fact, the root of all sin is doing what *we* want to do, doing what *we* think is right. This was Eve's sin in the garden.

God alone determines right and wrong, not we ourselves. Hell is filled with people who are convinced of their own morality. Scripture teaches that to disagree with God is immorality itself.

Consequently, deceit can be quite moral when it serves God's purposes. We have to be very careful here because of the human tendency to justify our own actions. However, when the enemy shows up at your door he does not deserve the truth. For instance, protecting Jews from the Nazis was morally good even when it required deceit and lies. These are the hard realities of life that make biblical judgment and discernment difficult. Fortunately, such situations are rare.

For the most part Paul captured the essence of this commandment when he wrote, "Let all bitterness and wrath and anger and tumult and evil speaking be put away from you, with all malice. And be kind to one another, tenderhearted, forgiving one another, even as God for Christ's sake has forgiven you" (Ephesians 4:31-32).

Most of what we call slander comes from these things—wrath, anger, tumult, and malice. Slander consists of saying false and malicious things about people that damage their reputation or well being. Even while protecting Jews against the Nazis, Christians should refrain from wrath, anger, and malice. We must love our enemies in spite of everything, and not respond to them with anger or malice. Living in the service of God's purposes does not justify such things, even in the face of obvious evil.

Jesus respected Pilate's position, authority, and person in spite of the evil he represented. He did not respond to Pilate with anger or malice. James reminds us that we are not to stand in judgment of God's law, but to be obedient to it in all things. "Do not speak against one another, brothers. He who speaks against his brother, and who judges his brother, speaks against the Law and judges the Law. But if you judge the Law, you are not a doer of the Law, but a judge" (James 4:11).

To live as a Christian is a high calling. It is not easy or cheap. It requires diligence and discernment, faithfulness and commitment, obedience and courage.

PRACTICAL APPLICATION

The practical application of the Ninth Commandment involves working to love and protect the reputations of our neighbors. The Larger Catechism explains:

> The duties required in the ninth commandment are, the preserving and promoting of truth between man and man, and the good name of our neighbor, as well as our own; appearing and standing for the truth; and from the heart, sincerely, freely, clearly, and fully, speaking the truth, and only the truth, in matters of judgment and justice, and in all other things whatsoever.

Here we see that even the catechism leans toward turning this Commandment into a platitude. It is essentially correct in that it explains that we are to make every effort to be truthful, to know the truth, and to tell the truth to the very best of our ability. And that we are to tell God's truth—because there is no other. We are, however, not to err in our efforts to be truthful apart from discerning the will of God. Scripture must always be our guide, not what we ourselves believe to be true apart from Scripture. This advice from the catechism has difficulty defending Rahab's faithfulness because it over generalizes the lesson it draws from Scripture.

The Catechism question 144 goes on to say that we should have:

> a charitable esteem of our neighbors; loving, desiring, and rejoicing in their good name; sorrowing for, and covering of their infirmities; freely acknowledging of their gifts and graces, defending their innocence; a ready receiving of a good report, and unwillingness to admit of an evil report, concerning them; discouraging tale-bearers, flatterers, and slanderers; love and care of our own good name, and defending it when need requireth; keeping of lawful promises; studying and practicing of whatsoever things are truth, honest, lovely, and of good report.

Indeed, we are to be honest and truthful, but not at the expense of God's written and express purposes. Again, we must heed a serious caution in this regard because of our ability to justify our own actions. Absolute dependence upon the Word of God and His Holy Spirit is essential in this regard. Thus, not only are God's people to be honest and truthful in all things, but also are to have discernment of God's will and discretion regarding God's purposes. Christians must always be engaged in the faithful service of their Lord.

DESIRE

You shall not covet your neighbor's house. You shall not covet your neighbor's wife, nor his manservant, nor his maidservant, nor his ox, nor his ass, nor anything that is your neighbor's. —Exodus 20:17

The Tenth Commandment encapsulates the heart of the law, and in this regard it is somewhat different than the other commandments. It is the most general of the commandments. Jeremiah 17:9 notes that the "heart is deceitful above all things, and desperately wicked." The Tenth Commandment is aimed directly at the deceitful human heart. It demands, not merely a purity of action, but a purity of intent. God demands that the intentions of His people be pure according to His Word. The desires of His people must accurately reflect His own desires as those desires are articulated in the Bible.

The truth of the gospel is not that Christians have conquered the sinful nature of their own hearts, but that they are more aware of their own sin and guilt than others are. Christians do not exist in a state of constant happiness because they have been purged of sin. Rather, Christians are painfully aware of their own sins because of the gospel of God's grace and mercy. They are not left with the awareness of their sin. That awareness is not all there is to being a Christian. But the fullness of Christianity necessarily rests upon this foundation. The gospel frees God's people from the ignorance of their own sin, but requires the awareness of sin. In the light of their own sin, believers are saved by their faith in Christ's righteousness. Redeemed sinners are saved, but they remain sinners. What Christian is above Saint Paul in this regard?

Paul delighted "in the law of God according to the inward man" (Romans 7:22), but witnessed another law functioning in his members. His spirit and flesh warred against each other, not only after he was saved, but *because* he was saved. His salvation ignited that war. The commandment, the Word of God or the gospel of salvation, which God intended to be the foundation of life itself, became the foundation of death for Paul (Romans 7:10). Paul said that the gospel brought him death, the death of his ignorance of his own sinfulness, the death of the old man.

When Paul was saved, he discovered that he had been previously living in death because he had not been aware of his own sinfulness. Upon regeneration Paul became painfully aware of his own sin, that he had been living in death, living according the values of death, that his own life contributed toward the death of mankind. When God regenerated Paul, he saw himself as God saw him, as a sinner. He had never thought of himself as a sinner before the Lord changed His heart on the road to Emmaus.

The Lord showed him his own sin. When he realized that he stood condemned by the Lord for his sin, he was terrified, and threw himself into repentance. From that point on Paul strove to live as God demanded in everything. Salvation instilled in Paul a new set of values, a new way of life, which started a war against the law of his mind. He suddenly saw himself as God saw him—as a sinner. He suddenly realized that he had lived his whole life in "captivity to the law of sin" (Romans 7:23). He could no longer live as he had lived before. His life as a successful Pharisee was ruined, and upon those ruins God built a new life. This is the pattern for regeneration.

Paul was awakened from thinking that God was only concerned with outward behavior, as he had previously believed as a Pharisee, to the understanding that God demanded a purity of heart and mind that was completely beyond his own ability to achieve. Upon regeneration, Paul's wretchedness made Christ's righteousness crystal clear. Prior to his rebirth in Christ, Paul thought he had been pretty holy. His salvation did not simply make him happy, but brought him into personal despair about the condition of his own life apart from the righteousness of Christ.

That kind of personal despair is an endemic part of salvation. It is a necessary part of salvation. Salvation brings one's own sin into focus, and despair is the natural reaction. Where there is no such personal despair, there can be no realization of the depth and tenacity of sin, nor the unburdening of the weight of sin. The degree of despair, of course, is relative. People experience it differently. But the fact of this kind of despair is universal because of the universality of human sin. Only non-sinners can be free from it, and there aren't any.

The purpose of the Tenth Commandment is to break through the facade of personal righteousness and/or of moral neutrality, and reveal the heart of personal sinfulness by stressing, not outward behavior, but inward desire. Human sin is so pervasive that it affects not only outward actions, but it corrupts all our thoughts, desires, and intentions as well. It is one thing to control one's own behavior. But it is another thing entirely to control one's own desire. A person can refrain from some particular action, regardless of how he feels about it, but how can a person refrain from personal desire? Desires just happen. I like this, I don't like that. Why? Who knows? Yet the Tenth Commandment commands God's people to control their own desires.

"You shall not covet..." (Exodus 20:17). The Hebrew word is *chamad*, and means to desire, to delight, or to take pleasure in something. God demands that His people not enjoy a certain kind of proclivity, a certain kind of inclination, personal preference or desire, and the activity that accompanies it. In essence, He demands that His people not desire what He forbids. But is that something that people can control? Can people choose what they will or won't desire? It is an interesting question that does not yield a simple solution.

Desires, more than anything else, reveal character. Personal desires or preferences clearly reflect personal character. People are what they want, they become what they desire. But is personal desire something that we can control? Can people simply choose to want certain things, or to stop craving other things? Can people choose to *want* to follow Jesus? We know that some people choose to follow Jesus and some don't. We also know that no one chooses to follow the Lord unless they want to. But what causes one person to want to follow Christ and another not to have that desire?

Paul said that all people are "dead in trespasses and sins" (Ephesians 2:1) until they are regenerated by the Holy Spirit. That means that people are unable to want or desire to choose to follow Jesus until their hearts are renewed. God must act upon a person—change a person—before that person is even able to rightly discern or desire Him. Thus, whenever anyone truly desires to follow Jesus, we know that they can do so only by the power of the Holy Spirit. Thus, the love of Christ is a mark of the Holy Spirit.

We are to love Christ. We are to seek to please the Lord in all things. And that means that we are not to love or desire certain other things. When God commands, "You shall not covet..." we are thrown into a quandary. There are two sets of human desires that are mutually exclusive. The desires of the flesh and the desires of the Spirit cannot coexist. "For they who are according to the flesh mind the things of flesh, but they who are according to the Spirit the things of the Spirit" (Romans 8:5). Certain human desires—inclinations, preferences, choices, propensities—are forbidden. For instance, we are not to desire whatever belongs to our neighbor. We are not to want to be like our neighbors, or to have what they have. We are not to be jealous of what other people have. In other words, we are to be content with what we have, with what the Lord has given us.

The fact is that many of our own desires are not under our own control. To a certain extent people can control how they respond to their desires, but the desires themselves are given. They just are what they are! Aren't they? Consequently, to submit them to control means to submit them to some power beyond ourselves, ideally to God. Personal desires are given by God and corrupted by sin and by sin's author, Satan.

All of the original desires of human life were holy, but they were corrupted by Satan, and human sin continues to corrupt them in our ordinary experience. In any case, basic human desires, like character itself, lie outside of human control. That is exactly why God issued this commandment. Obedience to this commandment requires genuine and complete submission to God.

This commandment flies in the face of modern society and the beliefs and understandings of modern society in many ways. It certainly runs counter to the advertising media that so dominates our lives. The heart of modern society is commerce—business. Commercials drive our modern economy. Advertisements tend to stimulate the very things that the Tenth Commandment forbids.

It is not that Scripture forbids commerce, nor that it forbids technological development. Scripture is not against personal wealth or creativity or social living. God wants His people to be well off. He wants His people to live creative and happy social and productive lives. But He knows that the effort to do so apart from Him, apart from living as He commands, cannot bring these things about. To live apart from God is to bring death to society. So, God shows us the boundaries beyond which death lies. We call them the Ten Commandments.

For instance, Scripture forbids the kind of values that drive people into debt in order to have everything they want. The Tenth Commandment is a kind of social regulator of greed. Rampant greed will kill a society, so the Lord forbids the causes of greed. Covetousness and materialism are the root causes of greed and selfishness that will undermine and destroy the fabric of social trust that is necessary for healthy social interaction. Uncontrolled desire ignites a fire in the soul that cannot be contained. To want this and want that and to define your life by the things you want—even good things like homes, cars, and good jobs to pay for it all—is to live a life of covetousness. The Tenth Commandment which condemned Paul condemns the whole world, and our modern or postmodern world is no exception.

Does this mean that most people live covetous lives? It does. But this is not new. People have always been this way. That is why God instituted this commandment. What is different in our day is that our whole economy requires and stimulates covetousness as the foundation of its commerce. People no longer seek to satisfy their basic needs, but seek to satisfy their every desire. The Lord aimed the Tenth Commandment at curbing this tendency.

"For the nations seek after all these things" (Matthew 6:32), said Jesus. Matthew uses the Hebrew word *goyim*, which means non-Jewish people, and is here translated as *nations*. From a New Testament perspective it refers to unsaved people. "For your heavenly Father knows that you have need of all these things. But seek first the kingdom of God and His righteousness; and all these things shall be added to you" (Matthew 6:31-32). Christians must not be unconcerned about "these things." Christians are to live life well, and in order to do that we must put God, God's Word and God's law, above our personal desires. Obedience must be more important than personal comfort. The love of the Lord must be more important than houses, cars, money, lifestyles, friends, family, governments—everything.

Does the application of this commandment require the abandonment of modern society? Not entirely. The evils from which we suffer are not the result of modern technology, but are the result of unrepentant hearts. The problem is not technology, but sin. There is nothing that sinful people cannot abuse, nor anything from which redeemed people cannot benefit. The problem is not other people, nor is it modern technology. The problem is sin, and only God has the remedy. The remedy is salvation in Christ, and the reengagement of the Ten Commandments in the righteousness of Christ. There is no other way.

SCRIPTURE INDEX

Books by Phillip A. Ross

It's About Time! — The Time Is Now

40 pages. 2008.

This book is about thinking about God, the gospel, and Jesus Christ. We all need to make more time to do that. It is for the Mid-Ohio River Valley, but it is also for every valley where people live. It comes to a valley perspective from a valley perspective. This booklet is not about a mountaintop experience nor is it from a mountaintop perspective. Rather, it is from the "street," down in the valley where people actually live. It is not sad or morose, but it is serious—and it's about sin, yours and mine. It is an invitation to think more deeply about the things that we deeply care about, the things we believe. It's about Jesus.

These essays were originally written in 1998 as a short sermon series during Advent. They are not the usual Advent presentation of well-worn platitudes and biblical pablum. Unlike too many of my peers, I can't stomach that kind of stuff. To me, warm milk not only tastes bad, but it makes me sleepy.

This booklet is about the time in which we live. Hopefully, you will find it to be timely in your own life, as well. Time is a funny thing. We all live in it. Most of us are slaves to it, driven by appointments and schedules that must be kept. Asking people to think about time is like asking a fish to think about water—with one important difference. As far as we know, fish can't think at all, at least not in the way that we define thinking. I will ask you to think about time, about how much time you have, how much you need, and what you do with it.

Engagement—Establishing Relationship in Christ

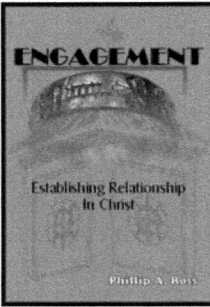

104 pages, 1996, 2008.

The material in this book is not my usual fare, but was an attempt to put my best understanding of Scripture and salvation in Christ into a succinct format for a church that did not know me. It is not a expositional book study, but is more of a topical study intended to speak to the needs of contemporary people by uncovering various biblical truths and at the same time revealing various contemporary misunderstandings about the Bible and salvation.

As you will come to understand, it created quite a stir among those who heard it. But it did not generate church renewal or revival, at least not in the way that anyone would notice, not in what are considered to be the measures of renewal and revival. Rather, many hearers found it quite disturbing, and I then found myself in defensive mode as it seems to have raised more questions that it answered.

What you will see here is a synopsis of the historic, Protestant, Reformed position. If it seems unusual it is more likely because this theological position has been all but abandoned by the vast majority of contemporary Christians and their churches over the past 20, 50 or 100 years, depending on where you live and what circles you fellowship in.

The Big Ten—A Study of the Ten Commandments

105 pages, 2001, 2008.

We live in an age of increasing lawlessness. It is not simply that there is a void of law, far from it. Quite the opposite is actually true. There is an over-whelming preponderance of laws, the size, scope and complexity of which world has never before seen. The body of law for any modern country, and in particular the United States—the most litigious society in history—is phenomenal. So, how can I say that we live in an age of increasing lawlessness?

What is in view here is not human law, but God's law. Just to speak the phrase brings a chill upon many a backbone. People don't like to talk about God's law. To do so is to be branded a fundamentalist, legalist, theonomist and/or extremist, all in the most vile sense of the words. For the most part contemporary Christians believe that they have arrived at a time in history that is beyond the application of any Old Testament laws, and in many cases, a time that is beyond all biblical law. People have converted the gospel of grace to mean a gospel without law—without obligation or responsibility.

The good news that is preached in too many pulpits today is lawlessness, couched in terms of a gospel of positive thinking, of upbeat moralisms intended to make life better, richer, fuller, more meaningful, and happier. In order to justify the human distaste for biblical law, people—Christians among them—no longer speak of God's law or the human obligation to it, not even in Bible study or worship.

However, the Bible is not a divided witness. It is a whole, a unity. God's Word, God's testimony is completely true.

THE WISDOM OF JESUS CHRIST IN THE BOOK OF PROVERBS

414 pages, 2006.

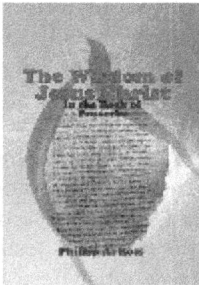

This study of Proverbs is an attempt to uncover the biblical message of Proverbs verse by verse in the light of Jesus Christ. We cannot pretend to be other than Christians who live on the redemption side of the Cross, while Proverbs was written on the anticipation side of the Cross. Nonetheless, the Christian faith is founded on the eternal consistency of God. God does not change. The God of Solomon, the author (and editor) of Proverbs, is the same God spoken of in the New Testament. In fact, the God of Solomon is Jesus Christ by the power of the Holy Spirit. Thus, the present work acknowledges this fact of faith and applies it by reading Proverbs in the light of Jesus Christ.

MARKING GOD'S WORD—UNDERSTANDING JESUS

324 pages, 2006.

Contemporary Western churches are a wreck, regardless of denominational affiliation or lack thereof. Mainline churches have been in serious decline for 50 years. The so-called contemporary churches are simply picking up transfer growth from other churches. Saying that there is a problem is one thing, but clearly defining the problem is something else. That something else is the subject of Marking God's Word. Clearly, there is much confusion in and out of the church about Christianity. Is confusion about the gospel of Jesus Christ new to the Modern and/or Postmodern world? That is the question that has haunted this treatment of Mark. *Marking God's Word* will help you see the gospel with new eyes, from a perspective that is obscured by sin and selfishness. Yet, this is not a new perspective. Rather, it is an old perspective that has a long and noble history of reformation and revival. Come, see Christ again, for the first time.

ACTS OF FAITH—KINGDOM ADVANCEMENT

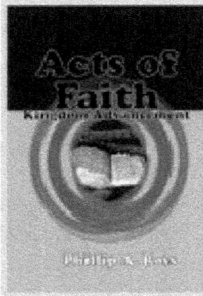

326 pages, 2007.

Acts of the Apostles continues the story of Jesus after His death. The story of the misunderstanding of the gospel among those who personally knew Jesus continues in the ministry of Paul. Paul, who was knocked off his high horse and thrown to the ground against his will and born again by the power of the Holy Spirit, came to see that he had been completely blind, and had his eyes miraculously opened. Paul – formerly the chief enemy of Christ, who became the chief disciple—took up the ministry and perspective of Jesus and began preaching the message of Christ to anyone who would listen. But Paul had the same difficulties that Jesus had—people thought he was crazy, that he didn't know what he was talking about, that he had gotten the gospel mes-sage wrong. Paul was hounded to death by the enemies of Christ, just as Jesus had been. Again, what is discovered in Acts of Faith is not a new perspective on Paul, but a very old one—the forgotten perspective of God's remnant.

INFORMAL CHRISTIANITY—REFINING CHRIST'S CHURCH

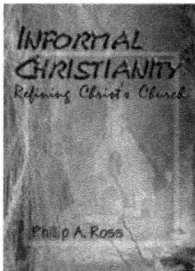

136 pages, 2007.

Informal Christianity reviews the personal and informal realities involved in a personal relationship with Jesus Christ that provide the foundation of Christianity. Where the internal and subjective realities of regeneration are absent from the lives of church members, churches find themselves on a foundation of sand. Such churches turn away from the heart of Christianity — doctrine and theology — to focus on peripheral concerns of administra-

tion and maintenance. Christians and churches that do not enthusias-
tically embrace biblical doctrine and theology as the life-blood of faithfulness, tend to spend their time and energy polishing the outside of
the cup (Matthew 23:25). Such efforts concern themselves with church
growth — noses and nickels — rather than Christian maturity
(Ephesians 4:13).

Informal Christianity aims to drive a nail through the heart of such
trivial indulgence on the part of those who fail to live up to the potential of their Christian calling because such a failure amounts to the
denial of the power and presence of the Holy Spirit in their own lives.
Yes, the flesh is weak, no one is disputing that. But "the spirit indeed
is willing" (Matthew 26:41). Christians "receive power when the Holy
Spirit has come upon" (Act 1:8) them. Such power is the "strength that
God supplies" (1 Peter 4:11). To wallow in administrative trivialities is
to deny the power of God (Mark 12:24) and to deny one's citizenship in
the Kingdom of God.

While great effort is being poured into the administrative expan-
sion of churches (church growth), the very heart of personal faithfulness is being ignored, denied, denigrated and trivialized by the very
principles that have been adopted to generate such growth. The
proper priorities and first things (Matthew 6:33) are giving way to the
"wisdom of men" (1 Corinthians 2:5). Informal Christianity cuts
through the trees that have become veritable logs in the eyes of
contemporary Christians to reveal again the forest of faithfulness in
which the life of Christianity dwells.

PRACTICALLY CHRISTIAN—APPLYING JAMES TODAY

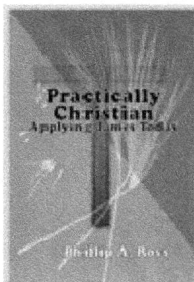

135 pages, 2006.

Practically Christian offers a fresh and insightful
application of the ancient Christian epistle of
James to the contemporary American Evangelical
world. Against the Antinomian backdrop of a
Christianity shaped by the Church Growth Movement, Practically Christian puts teeth into Christianity, pressing for a practical realism in order to
re-store some theological balance and sanity to
the practice of the faith.

*"Practically Christian offers a fresh and insightful
application of the ancient Christian epistle to the contemporary American
evangelical world. Against the Antinomian backdrop of a Christianity shaped
by the church growth movement, Ross puts teeth into Christianity, pressing
for a practical realism in order to restore some theological balance and sanity.*

His book is by no means dull reading or trite, but is replete with fresh anec-dotes illustrating the salient points he is conveying. I found his exposition of James 1:2-4 to be especially instructive and profound, and on that basis alone the book was worth reading. Ross's commitment to Reformed doctrine is quite obvious throughout. Many parts of the book I wish I had written myself!"
                                    —David C. Brand, Pastor and author

ARSY VARSY—RECLAIMING THE GOSPEL

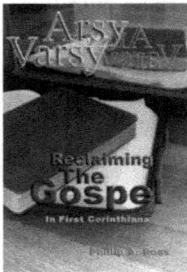

436 pages, 2008.
"Corinth was a city of wealth and culture, seated at the crossroads of the Roman Empire, where all the trade and commerce of the empire passed through. It was a city of beauty, a resort city, located in a very beautiful area, but it was also a city of prostitution and of passion. It was devoted to trade and commerce, but also to the worship of the goddess of sex" (*The Corinthian Crisis*, by Ray Steadman).

Paul had a problem with the Christians at Corinth. They were a large, successful church. They were growing leaps and bounds. They thought they were doing great. But not Paul. Paul found that they had substituted the wisdom of the world (the philosophy and culture of the Greeks) for the wisdom of Christ (the philosophy and culture of the Bible). This volume contrasts the folly of Greek (and ultimately modern American) worldly wisdom with the gospel of Christ. Stones are turned over and small-minded creatures that thrive in the dark scatter in the light of Christ.

Ross brings Paul's struggle to light with clarity and passion that leaves the worldly no where to hide in this panoptic treatment to First Corinthians.

VARSY ARSY—PROCLAIMING THE GOSPEL IN SECOND CORINTHIANS

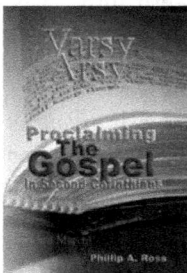

356 pages, 2009.
Paul continued the same thrust of his criticism and correction in his Second Letter to the Corinthians, apparently because the same problems continued to dog the church. Paul's Second Letter is more personal as he ramped up the tone and clarity of his criticism. At one point he thought that he may have overstepped the bounds of propriety and apol-ogized for his curtness—but not for his correction.

Personal attacks against Paul, against him personally and the style and content of his ministry, had continued. So, Paul addressed them with clarity and severity.

The Jews and the Greeks provided substantial difficulties for Paul's ministry. But worse than those who had blatantly refused to conform to the light of Christ were those who disguised themselves as apostles of Christ, those who thought that they were helping the cause of Christianity by redefining it to fit into their own ill-conceived ideas. Apparently, the errant Corinthian leaders had been involved in these kinds of creative adaptations of the gospel. As much as Jesus had opposed the Pharisees, Paul opposed the false apostles. Both were guilty of perverting the doctrines and wisdom of Scripture.

Before we think that this idea is impossible because it is so outrageous, we need to realize that this *modus operandi* is not at all unusual. Satan's methodology has always been to counterfeit the truth because he has no truth or light himself. Satan goes the extra mile to make his wisdom look like Christ's wisdom—and many people are fooled by it (Matthew 24:24, 2 John 1:7), "as the serpent deceived Eve by his cunning" (2 Corinthians 11:3). It's the same old same old, a different instance of the same thing.

Against this backdrop, Paul clarified and reclaimed the true gospel, bringing to light many of the common errors that continue to haunt the church in our own day.

Books can be purchased at your favorite bookstore, on the Internet at www.pilgrim-platform.org or by calling 877-805-0676.